Wind in the Sail

by

Robin Dinnanauth

Preface

The word "wind" comes from the Latin word ***"ventus"*** meaning the perceptible natural movements of the air, especially in the form of a current of air blowing from a particular direction or point. Wind is a major agent in determining the weather as well as the psychological environment of our mind. Wind can be extremely powerful. The wind has the power to broadcast seed and disperse spore, damage soil through erosion.

Having ***"wind in the sail"*** is the same that has been on a roll and it means to have some impetus or to be fired up to do something. Biblically, it means having some difficulties in our life or our day-to-day activities as well as having some moments of joy, restoration, or refreshing in our lives. Mankind generally has difficulty in controlling or harnessing the wind, that is why God Almighty controls and direct or channels the wind through an invisible medium, thereby making it an ideal symbol for God's Holy Spirit. Biblically, mankind has difficulty and hindrances in their daily activities. However, God has the sovereign power to solve this difficulty or hindrance for us because we are His people. He, in His supreme nature, has the ultimate power to save mankind from every wind that we are passing through in our lives or our daily endeavors.

In following Christ, we must strive to imitate Him. ***"He that followeth me shall not walk in darkness, saith the Lord."*** These are the words of Christ, and this teaches us how far we must imitate His life and character if we seek true spiritual awareness and deliverance from all evil attack. His teaching surpasses all teachings of Holy men and His Spirit is noticed in this hidden manner. There are many who, though they frequently hear the gospel, have little longing for it, this is because they do not have the mind of Christ. He, therefore, who willfully and with true knowledge, perceives the words of Christ, let him try to evolve his whole life to the mind of Christ. It is vanity to seek after and also to trust in the riches that shall perish. It is vainness too to covet honors and to lift up ourselves high. It is vainness to follow the wishes of the flesh and be led by them, for this shall bring misery at the end. It is vainness to want an extended life and to possess very little care for an honest life. It is vainness to require thought just for the life now.

Vain is the life of that man who puts his trust in men or in any created things. Be not humiliated to be the servant of others for the love of the Savior and to be reckoned as poor in this life. Rest not upon thyself, however, build thy hope in God. Do what lies in God's power and God will help your good intent. Trust neither in thy learning nor in the cleverness of any lives, but rather trust in the favor of God who resists the proud and gives grace to the humble. There is no man who is altogether free from temptations, as he lives as a result of the basis of temptation inside ourselves, in that we are born in concupiscence. As one temptation or sorrow passes, another comes; we always have somewhat to suffer. This is because we have fallen from perfect happiness. Many who request to fly from temptations fall, however, a lot are deeply into them. By flight alone, we tend not to overcome; however, by endurance and true humility, we are stronger than all our enemies.

Table of Contents

Chapter 1

The Spiritual Wind:
It's Meaning and How We Face It
in Our Daily Living

S cripturally, wind means either lack of substances, means of adversity, or changeableness. Winds in the scripture have negative or positive meaning. In the negative aspect, wind could either be a hardship, misfortune, a delay or disappointment, a plague or unpleasant situation, a reproach facing an individual or a group of people. In the positive aspect, it could be good news, restoration of lost blessings or miracle, deliverance from sickness or evil attack, answer to one prayer, a season of pleasant breakthroughs, or uplifting experience by an individual or a group of people at large. It is only when these pictures of wind connect to the person of God that we find more positive meanings.

Spiritually, mankind as a whole, face in one way or another different kinds of wind in our daily living. One of the characteristics of wind is that it can damage soil over time. It has the capacity of moving sand from a particular region to another; likewise, our lives are faced with different challenges. Job, a man in the land of Uz, was an upright and perfect man who feared God and hated evil. He was wealthy and also great as a result of his uprightness with God. But when the wind of life blew on him, he lost virtually everything he possessed including his children.

> *"While he was however speaking, there came also another, and said, thy sons and thy daughters were eating and drinking wine in their eldest brother's house. And behold, there came an excellent wind from the geographical area and smote the four corners of the house, and it fell upon the young men, and they are dead and I solely am at large alone to inform thee." (Job 1:18–19 KJV)*

A second and more encouraging aspect of the wind is its independence. Wind appears almost to be impulsive or whimsical. By the virtue of its strength and its unpredictable changeableness, it frustrates mankind. It leaves mankind wondering and pondering on what is next, thereby making us seek refuge or go into hiding. The wind presents difficulties that are beyond the power of man. Elimelech's life is a good example of this. Elimelech was a man from Judah who, because of the famine in the land, went into the country of Moab to sojourn with them and also seek for shelter, but he ended up losing his life and that of his two sons who went into the country with him, thereby making his wife, Naomi, a widow.

> *"And Elimelech, Naomi's husband, died; and she was left, and her two sons. And they took them wives of the women of Moab; the name of the one was Orpah and the name of the other Ruth: and they dwelt there about ten years. And Mahlon and Chilion died both of them; and the woman was left of her two children and of her husband." (Ruth 1:3–5)*

A third encouraging aspect of the wind is that God created the wind; He controls it. Spiritually, in our lives today as mankind, there are certain challenges or hardships that were put into our lives by God for Him to be glorified in it. The experience of the disciples on the ship is a good example of this.

> *"He saith unto them, 'Why are ye fearful, O ye of little faith?' Then he arose, and rebuked the winds and the sea; and there was a great calm. But the men marveled, saying 'What manner of man is this, that even the winds and the sea obey him!'" (Matthew 8:26–27 KJV)*

Wind is invisible, we cannot see it. Generally, mankind nowadays is faced with one problem or pleasant experiences or others that we do not know of. Some of these problems or pleasant experiences are inherited ones; some are results of the activities of the wicked ones in

2

our lives. Some of us today are proud to be called by the surname we are bearing because it's a well-known one, which is a result of the labor of grace that has been made available to us by our forefathers. Spiritually, our salvation made available by God was by grace. God sent His only Son who had no sin, who was sinless, to pay the debt He didn't owe. Our salvation was a result of the grace of God that we enjoyed.

> *"For it is by grace you have been saved, through faith—and this is not from yourselves, it is the gift of God—not by works, so that no one can boast." (Ephesians 2:8–9)*

Wind is a good word to describe the power of the Holy Spirit. The word "wind" comes from "*pnoe*," which describes the wind that is so loud that one may be tempted to cover his ears from the mighty noise of it. This was indicated whenever the Spirit was poured out, it was never a quiet affair. The wind was loud, noisy, violent, and strongly felt. The wind moves ships, empowers engines, drives windmills, and disperses pollution from the Earth. This is evident when the Holy Spirit moved on the Day of the Pentecost; He released power strong enough to transform 120 disciples into a mighty force for God. When the wind of the Spirit blows upon a nearly dead church, it can blow life back into that congregation again. When you desire a "quiet" relationship with God, the Holy Spirit's wind blows—it is rarely a quiet affair. Wind is always noisy and attention-grabbing; a powerful force that sweeps downward from heaven like the roaring of the sea.

When man was created, God created him perfectly. But the man had no breath in his lungs until God breathed the breath of life into him *(see Genesis 2:7)*. Likewise, when the church was gathered together on the Day of Pentecost, there was no power until the Holy Spirit breathed into that congregation. When the loud *"boom"* exploded overhead in the room where they were gathered, the power of God came upon 120 disciples, and they became an empowered, mighty force on earth. When winds blow, change happens; and when the Holy Spirit moves, He brings change like the mighty wind. Energy

3

is produced by wind and when the Holy Spirit moves, He supplies supernatural energy. The Holy Spirit empowers us to do what we could naturally not do on our own. All we need is the supernatural wind of the Holy Spirit.

The word "wind" symbolizes an effective power, but it belonged wholly to the realm of nature. In all of these, wind remains an impersonal, natural force. Wind serves as a symbol of transience *(Psalm 78:39)*, fruitless striving *(Ecclesiastes 1:14)*, and desperateness *(Job 6:26)*. More importantly, it is a mighty force which only God could command *(Jeremiah 10:13)*. The wind does God's bidding *(Psalm 104:4)*. The wind is closely connected with God's will that it is called His "breath," which He blew on the sea to cover the chariots of the pharaoh *(Exodus 15:10)*, by which He froze rivers *(Job 37:10)* and withered grass *(Isaiah 40:7)*.

In the Old Testament, the primary meaning of the word *"ruach"* is wind. There is the slight breeze *(Psalm 78:39)*, the storm wind *(Isaiah 32:2)*, the whirlwind *(2 Kings 2:11)*, and the scorching wind *(Psalm 11:6)*. Winds that blow from the mountains and sea to the north and west bring rain and storm *(1 Kings 18: 43–45; Exodus 10:19; Ezekiel 1:4)*; those coming from the deserts of the south and east are, at times, balmy but more often would sear the land and dry up the vegetation *(Genesis 41:6; Job 37:1–2)*. Wind was identified by the directions from which they emanate, making references to the four corners or quarters of the earth or of heaven *(Jeremiah 49:36; Ezekiel 37:9)*. The manifestations of God's power were often associated with the wind. God answered Job out of the windstorm *(Job 38:1)*, and the four living creatures appeared to Ezekiel in a strong wind from the north *(Job 1:4)*.

The wind was the breath in humans as the breath of life *(Genesis 6:17)*. The entry of the wind, which symbolizes breath gives life *(Ezekiel 37:5–7)*, and, when taken away, the person dies *(Psalm 104:29)*. The breath that brings death, when taken away, is identified as God's breath *(Job 34:14-15)*. This same breath of the Almighty is the spirit of wisdom and understanding bestowed upon the individual *(Job 32:8)*. When *ruah* is used of the will, intellect, and emotions, or related to God, the meaning often expands from the wind to the spirit

(Isaiah 40:13). Thus, *ruah* was used in Psalm 51:1 three times when referring to the steadfast, willing, and broken spirit of the psalmist, and once when speaking of God's Holy Spirit *(Psalm 51:10–12; Psalms 51:10–12, 51:17)*. The meaning is best served by translating the word as *"wind"* (breath) or *"spirit"* when it is specifically assigned to the truth of God. In the New Testament, God makes His angels *winds (Hebrews 1:7)*, and *"with the breath of His mouth,"* the Lord Jesus will destroy the wicked one *(2 Thessalonians 2:8)*.

The wind or breath of God signifies the life that belongs to heaven and to the man who is in heaven—one who is regenerate. The evidence can be seen in these passages:

> *"By the Word of the Lord were the heavens made; and all the army of heaven by the breath [wind] of his mouth." (Psalm 33:6 BBE)*

> *"Thou takest their breath, they expire and return to their dust. Thou sendest forth Thy spirit [wind], they are created." (Psalm 104:29–30 DBY)*

> *"He said unto me…can these bones live?*
> *Then said He, Prophesy unto the wind, prophesy, son of man, and say to the wind, Thus saith the Lord God, Come from the four winds, O breath, and breathe upon these slain, that they may live…and the breath came into them, and they lived." (Ezekiel 37:3, 9–10 KJV)*

> *I saw four angels standing upon the four corners of the earth, holding back the four winds of the earth that no wind should blow upon the earth nor upon the sea nor upon any tree." (Revelation 7:1 JUB)*

The spiritual meaning of winds also denotes "the life of heaven" which is "Divine life." These can be seen in Job: "The spirit of God hath made me, and the breath of Shaddai hath vivified me" (Job

33:4). Therefore, when the Lord teaches about the regeneration of man, He says:

> *"The spirit [or wind] bloweth where it listeth, and thou hearest the sound thereof, but canst not tell whence it cometh, and whither it goeth: so is every one that is born of the Spirit." (John 3:8 KJV)*

> *"Jehovah...breathed into his nostrils the breath of life; and Man became a living soul." (Genesis 2:7 DBY)*

Through the nostrils, respiration is effected, and through respiration, there is Divine life as in these passages:

> *"Cease ye from man, whose breath is in his nostrils." (Isaiah 2:22 ASV)*

> *"The breath of our nostrils, the anointed of Jehovah, was taken in their pits; of whom we said, Under his shadow we shall live among the nations." (Lamentations 4:20 DBY)*

The wind also signifies the presence of the Lord, and wherever the Lord is, evils and falsities are cast into hell, therefore the presence of the Lord is signified by the wind of the nostrils of God in these passages:

> *"And the beds of the sea were seen, The foundations of the world were uncovered. At the rebuke of Jehovah, at the blast of the breath of His nostrils." (2 Samuel 22:16 DBY)*

> *"The breath of the Lord, like a stream of sulfur, kindles it." (Isaiah 30:33 NRSV)*

> *"He sendeth His word, and melteth them; he causeth his wind to blow—the waters flow." (Psalms 147:18 DBY)*

The Bible makes references to four winds, which are powerful and figurative. There are four corners of the earth and these are four different directions the wind can blow to or from. These four winds can practically give life (Ezekiel 37:9) or scatter, uproot or destroy people, empires, kingdoms, etc. (Daniel 7:2, 8:8, 11:4; Zechariah 2:6; Jeremiah 49:36; Hosea 12:1; Revelation 7:1). Daniel 2:35 WBT gives us a glimpse of the power of the wind: "Then was the iron, the clay, the brass, the silver, and the gold, broken to pieces together, and became just like the chaff of the summer threshing-floors; and the wind carried them away, that no place was found for them." The wind has the power to carry anything, no matter how big or heavy it is. The four winds are summoned together and it breathes life into the slain so that they may live (Ezekiel 37:9). We shall later consider them separately.

Properties of the Wind

Wind is moving air; it is needed continually for life itself. Seeds usually need wind for its dissemination and subsequent growth. The Holy Spirit is the presence of God, the source for all life. It is invisible, the source or the destination of wind cannot be seen. It is a mysterious, unseen force and its presence is known by its effects. The unseen hypostasis may be better in an exceedingly refreshing approach. His presence is displayed in human lives through His works by teaching, transforming, sanctifying, and encouraging.

Wind is a powerful force which cannot be stopped or controlled by humans. Likewise, hypostasis isn't subject to human management. God at work shows the moving of the Holy Spirit. Wind is in great variety, which may be a soft whisper gently rustling or hurricane uprooting trees. The same applies to the Holy Spirit, gently bringing a person to Christ through conviction and conversion of the hardened sinner.

The Four Winds

> *"And after these things I saw four angels standing on the four corners of the earth, holding the four winds of the earth, that the wind should not blow on the planet, nor on the sea, nor on any tree." (Revelation 7:1 KJV)*

To understand how God uses the wind, we need knowledge of the two aspects of the wind. First, there are the natural or physical characteristics of the wind. Secondly, there are the spiritual characteristics of the wind. One spiritual characteristics of the wind is that it represents God's judgment. These spiritual winds of judgment are being held back from blowing on the earth until God has sealed the one hundred and forty-four thousand. Matthew speaks of God gathering His people after the wind of judgment blows upon the earth:

> *"And he shall send his angels with a great sound of a trumpet, and they shall gather together His elect from the four winds, from one end of heaven to the other." (Matthew 24:31 KJV)*

When God releases the four winds upon the earth at the time of His judgment, He will gather His people from these four winds. This will be a time of violence and turbulence never before seen by man. The Bible speaks of the North Wind, the South Wind, the East Wind, and the West Wind. Everything in God's Word has significance. The four directions have a religious significance. North is the direction of God's throne. It is the image of power, majesty, and authority. South is the direction of comfort, refreshment, and quietness. The easterly is the wind of judgment, which will blow before the New Day. The wind blows from the setting of the sun. The wind reveals the top of the day, or the end of an age, and the restoration of all things. As God's Word reveals the mysteries and the secrets of the four winds, we can begin to understand where we are in God's time table of the end-time events.

God determines when and which of the four winds will blow upon mankind.

Biblical Meaning of the Four Winds

The four winds are associated with the four corners of the earth or the four quarters of heaven. The four winds blow in all the direction of the earth. The power of the four winds is so tremendous in the Bible. The four winds can churn the great seas; it can uproot and scatter powerful empires. The four winds combined together in heaven were deployed against the nation of Elam to scatter the people in all directions.

The wind comes to us, we do not have to go the wind. The wind can be gentle like a pleasant breeze on a hot day or on a moonlit night. The wind can blow suddenly, as in a gust. The wind has great power. It can move clouds in the air and ship over the oceans and can drive turbines on land. The wind brings together air from distant places on earth. The wind may be like the spirit of God, but it is not God.

"Then was the iron, the clay, the brass, the silver, and the gold, broken to pieces together, and became like the chaff of the summer threshing floors; and the wind carried them away, that no place was found for them: and the stone that smote the image became a great mountain, and filled the whole earth." (Daniel 2:35 KJV)

The wind can carry anything, no matter how big or heavy it is. The four winds were known to assemble along and breathe life into the slain so they will live. These four winds bring upon us divine judgment ranging from war, famine, pestilence, the overthrow of kingdom, and the universal wreck of all earthly things. There are various flows of this wind. The wind flows in a different direction. The wind of persecution; the wind of false doctrine; the wind of delusion and wild fanaticism; the wind of temptation; the wind of infidelity; the wind of open vocalization and blasphemy; the winds of affliction, adversity, and distress—by all of which the Church is frequently assailed. These things are known as "winds" because they produce agitation and commotion —breaking the branches, blasting the fruits,

9

and uprooting the trees of God's spiritual vineyard. They are known as "four" winds to show their universality, their wide-spreading desolation. They are called winds of the "earth" because the earth is the scene of their operation — they are forever excluded from heaven; their coming from the four cardinal points right away shows their violence, rage, and fury.

The four winds symbolize political commotion, strife, and war. The four winds, held by four angels standing in the four quarters of the earth, must denote all the elements of strife and commotion that exist in the world; and when they are all loosened, all blow together. "And after these things I saw four angels standing on the four corners of the earth, holding the four winds of the earth, that the wind should not blow on the earth, nor on the sea, nor on any tree" Revelation 7:1 KJV).

> *"Daniel spake and said, I saw in my vision by night, and, behold, the four winds of the heaven strove upon the great sea." (Daniel 7:2 KJV)*

Four mighty angels are still holding the four winds of the world. Terrible destruction is to come in full. The accidents by land and by sea; the loss of life steadily increasing, by storm, by tempest, by railroad disaster, by conflagration. The terrible floods, the earthquakes, and the winds stir the nations to at least one deadly combat while the angels hold the four winds, forbidding the terrible power of Satan to be exercised in its fury till the servants of God are sealed in their foreheads. The ministers of revenge can pour all the terrible judgments upon a God-desolate folks. The method of obedience is that the sole path of life. May the Lord help you to see it in time to open your ears, so that you may hear what the Spirit saith unto the churches. These winds are in check till God provides the word to allow them to go. There is the safety of God's church. The angels of God do His bidding, holding back the winds of the earth, so that the winds should not blow on the earth, nor on the sea, nor on any tree until the servants of God should be sealed in their foreheads. The mighty angel is seen ascending from the east (or the sun rising). This mightiest of angels has in his hand the seal of the living God or of immortality—eternal life. It is the voice of this highest angel that has authority to command the four angels to keep the four winds in check until this work is performed, and until He gives the summons to let them loose. The great day of God is hastening greatly. But though the nations are mustering their forces for war and bloodshed, the command to the angels remains good—that they hold the four winds till the servants of God are sealed in their foreheads

The four winds are spirit beings, the Creator's messengers that were placed at the four corners of the world at the beginning of time by the Creator. The task of the "bearer" is to attend to the cycle of the four seasons of the year. The messengers mind the movement of the sun, earth, and stars and charged with the responsibility of keeping a strict check up on the winds. Vigilance keeps all four winds from returning along and destroying living things on earth. In a continual state of action night and day, season through season, the bearers are given direction by the Creator regarding what they shall do and what actions they shall carry out for a particular season. It is part of their traditional instruction that has been told by the ancient priests that any individual who kills new meat shall take a part of the meat first to the priest. The priest cuts the meat into five sections, first giving a piece to the sacred fire located in the priest's house, then, in turn, throwing a piece to the winds of the north, south, east, and lastly, west. After this is completed, the meat is often passed as a whole through the sacred hearth and distributed among the families. The sun's earthborn presence is understood by the folks as the hearth through which the sun, the grandmother of all that lives, sees everything that happens on earth. Offerings are given to the bearer to appease them. The offering is given to the North Wind messenger, so he will not whine too long and destroy people with a cold. His color is black and his countenance stern. The giving is given to the wind traveler in order that he shouldn't send sturdy east winds to overturn the young corn once it comes into adornment or roasting ears time. His color is red and his countenance is congenial. The offering given to the South Wind will provide the people with good and mild winds which causes all things to grow. The giving is given to the wind traveler, an agency that frequently works to help his superior, the South Wind messenger. These two messengers together causes rains and bring water to the crops.

On occasion, the North Wind sends his great cold winds to blow between the West and the South Winds, but the West Wind always join with the South Wind and together, they blow the cold wind back. In summer, all three winds—the East, South, and West—join together against the North Wind to ensure that his cold winds do not invade and destroy living things. Sometimes the North Wind will go about in the night to blast fruit trees, gardens, the first small corn, and water. Because of the opposing three winds, he must do this very secretly. Since the North Wind messenger is capable of great mischief, the other winds are always on their guard against his tricks and keep him within boundaries. When people do wicked things, disobey their priests, and refuse to listen to their counsel, the Creator will set all four wind messengers against the earth to destroy crops and bring hunger to penalize individuals for his or her wicked actions.

The "four winds" in the Book of Revelation 7:1 are used in the context of judgment: "I saw four angels standing at the four corners of the earth, holding back the four winds" of the planet to stop any wind from blowing on the land or on the ocean or on any tree. This use of the "four winds" is different from other references because the winds are being held back rather than being sent forth. The holding back of the four winds represents the full theme of Revelation 7, which is a worshipful respite from the outpouring of God's judgments. The four winds that had antecedently painted destruction and affliction on the planet currently function the foremost as a moving and hope-filled promise from God for the protection of His people: "Do not damage the earth or the sea or the trees, until we have marked the servants of our God with a seal on their foreheads...and God will wipe away every tear from their eyes" (Revelation 7:3, 17 NRSV). The four winds are powerful, strong, and fierce in nature. There are four corners of the earth and these points are four different directions in which the wind can blow to or from. The four winds will provide life: "Then he said unto me, Prophesy unto the wind, prophesy, son of man, and say to the wind, Thus saith the Lord God; Come from the four winds, O breath, and breathe upon this slain, that they may live" (Ezekiel 37:9 KJV); or scatter, uproot, or destroy people, empires, kingdoms, *"Daniel spake and said, I saw in my vision by night, and, behold, the four winds of the heaven strove upon the great sea" (Daniel 7:2 KJV)*. "Therefore the he goat waxed very great: and when he was strong, the great horn was broken; and for it came up four notable ones toward the four winds of heaven" Daniel 8:8. Daniel 2:35 KJV gives us a glimpse of the power of the wind: *"Then was the iron, the clay, the brass, the silver, and the gold, broken to pieces together, and became like the chaff of the summer threshing floors; and the wind carried them away, that no place was found for them."*

The wind can carry anything, no matter how big, strong, large or heavy it is. The four winds were known to assemble along and breathe life into the slain in order that they will live

God's judgment is written in the wind; it is full of glorious revelations. God uses many things to explain His wonders He is performing on the earth. Most of God's followers are trying to find the profound, the miracle, the unexplainable, the experience, or the spiritual high; and they miss the simple truths and examples God has so wondrously shown us in His Word. The apostle Paul wrote: *"God hath chosen the foolish things of the world to confound the wise; and God hath chosen the weak things of the world to confound the things which are mighty" (1 Corinthians 1:27 KJV).*

God has chosen the foolish things of the globe to confound the wise. The words confound means "to disgrace and put to shame." God has chosen the foolish things of the world to disgrace and put to shame those who are walking after the flesh and not after the Spirit. He chose the weak things to dishonor and put to shame the things which are mighty. God will deal with the mighty in His own way. Because the mighty will not glorify God in their lives, God will disgrace and put them to shame: *"Because the foolishness of God is wiser than men; and the weakness of God is stronger than men" (1 Corinthians 1:25 KJV).*

God will show forth His power, His might, and His glory in those who have chosen to walk in His ways. Those who reject God's way will suffer the wrath. Apostle Paul wrote, *"For the invisible things of Him from the creation of the world are clearly seen, being understood by the things that are made, even his eternal power and Godhead; so that they are without excuse" (Romans 1:20 KJV).* Everything God created is a witness of His greatness and His eternal power. No one who has seen His creation will have any excuse for not knowing and recognizing their God. All who have witnessed the wonders of a tree, or smelled a rose, or wondered at the perfection of a newborn child will not have any excuse for denouncing their Creator God.

God's Treasure House

One of God's wonders of nature is the wind. All who live upon the earth have witnessed the wind from the gentle breeze to the gale winds, to the whirlwind, to the most violent typhoon. God speaks much about the wind in His Word. The prophet Jeremiah gave us insight into the wind: *"When He uttereth His voice, there is a multitude of waters in the heavens; and he causeth the vapou rs to ascend from the ends of the earth: he maketh lightnings with rain, and bringeth forth the wind out of his treasures" (Jeremiah 51:16 KJV).*

When God speaks of His treasures, they are the things of value that are stored until the time they are needed. He speaks of His treasures of the wind. The wind isn't the sole treasure God has in His treasury. Job also spoke of God's treasures: *"Hast thou entered into the treasures of the snow, and hast thou seen the treasures of the hail" (Job 38:22 KJV).* God conjointly has snow and hail in His treasures. God can use all His treasures, as it becomes necessary, to demonstrate His great power, authority, and majesty to those who inhabit the earth. The psalmist wrote: *"Fire, and hail; snow, and vapors; stormy wind fulfilling his word" (Psalm 148:8 WBT).* God has His treasure house full and is using this stored treasure to fulfill His Word. The day has come when God is releasing all His treasures in all their fury upon the earth.

There came a time when Jesus had to deal with the wind in His disciples' lives. After Jesus fed the five thousand, *"straightway he constrained his disciples to get into the ship, and to go to the other side before unto Bethsaida, while he sent away the people" (Mark 6:45 KJV). "And he saw them toiling in rowing; for the wind was contrary unto them: and about the fourth watch of the night he cometh unto them, walking upon the ocean, and would have passed by them" (Mark 6:48 KJV).*

The disciples were toiling in rowing, trying to get to where they wanted to go. But the wind was contrary unto them. Many today who think they are walking in the Spirit find the wind of the Lord is contrary to them. They are trying to get to where they want to go or do what they want to do. Jesus is always nearby, walking upon the sea, but He will continue to pass them by until they call out to Him. *"For they all saw him, and were troubled. And immediately he talked with them, and saith unto them, Be of good cheer: it is I; be not afraid. And he went up unto them into the ship; and the wind ceased: and they were sore amazed in themselves beyond measure, and wondered" (Mark 6:50–51 KJV).* The disciples were troubled when they saw Jesus. They thought they were all alone in their tribulation. They did everything humanly possible to solve their dilemma. It only took a word from the Lord, and their troubled sea was calm. There was another instance when Jesus's disciples were on the troubled sea, *"And, behold, there arose an excellent tempest within the ocean, insomuch that the ship was covered with the waves: but he was asleep. And his disciples came to him, and awoke him, saying, Lord, save us: we perish. And he saith unto them, Why are ye fearful, O ye of little faith? Then he arose, and rebuked the winds and the sea; and there was a great calm. But the men marveled, saying, What manner of man is this, that even the winds and the sea obey him" (Matthew 8:24–27 KJV).*

When you are going through the storms of life, you may think many times God is asleep or just simply not concerned about what you are going through? When our ship is covered with water and you think you are going to sink, this is when you desire to get God's attention. When everything is going well and you have smooth sailing ship, sometimes God gets in your way, and you would not care if He takes a nap and leave you alone. You are your own helmsman, and you do not need any help. But let the storm arise and your need for God arises very quickly, and you begin to seek His presence. The disciples got Jesus's attention, and He arose and rebuked the contrary wind in their lives, and there was a great calm. The peace that passes all understanding returned to their lives. When you are going through a difficult storm in your life, all you need is a word from the Lord and your storms become a great calm. You marvel, saying, "What manner of man is that this, that the wind and the sea obey Him." If the disciples had known the Word of God, they would not have been surprised because the psalmist wrote: *"He maketh the storm calm, so that the waves thereof are still" (Psalm 107:29 KJV).* When the wind of the Lord is contrary in your lives, then you are not going with the wind but contrary to the wind. You desire to go your own way; when the wind is contrary, the Lord is attempting to change your direction to walk with Him. When you change directions, then the wind will be at our backs and your sails will be full and our journey easy. When you are going against the wind, your toiling becomes impossible. When you call Christ into your ship and make Him your helmsman, you will reach His destination in your life.

The continual whirling North Wind and South Wind will calm our seas and bring the deliverance the Lord has promised. Praise will return to our lips, and joy will return to our heart. *"And I will be able to provide thee the treasures of darkness, and hidden riches of secret places, that thou mayest know that I, the Lord, which call thee by thy name, am the God of Israel" (Isaiah 45:3).*

The word darkness means "the place of obscurity," the secret place in God. The psalmist declared the secret place in God: *"He that dwelleth within the secret place of the most High shall abide under the shadow of the Almighty" (Psalm 91:1 KJV).* The secret place of the Highest God is His place of protection, the place of His hidden riches. This is God's treasure house for the people who love and serve Him. He has stored up His treasures for His use in the day of His wrath.

God is about to bring His wind out of His treasures. When the fullness of time has come, God's wind will blow as never before since the world began. Jesus revealed this mighty wind to John on the Isle of Patmos: *"After these things I saw four angels standing on the four corners of the earth, holding the four winds of the earth, that the wind should not blow on the earth, on the sea, nor on any tree" (Revelation 7:1 NKJV)*. To understand how God uses the wind, we need knowledge of the two aspects of the wind. First, there are the natural or physical characteristics of the wind. Secondly, there are the spiritual characteristics of the wind. One spiritual characteristic of the wind is that it represents God's judgment. These spiritual winds of judgment are being held back from blowing on the earth until God has sealed the one hundred and forty-four thousand. Matthew speaks of God gathering His people after the wind of judgment blows upon the earth: *"And he shall send his angels with a great sound of a trumpet, and they shall gather together his elect from the four winds, from one end of heaven to the other" (Matthew 24:31 KJV)*.

When God releases the four winds upon the world at the time of His judgment, He can gather His individuals from these four winds. This will be a time of violence and turbulence never before seen by man. The Bible speaks of Boreas, the wind, the East Wind, and the West Wind. Everything in God's Word has significance. The four directions even have a nonsecular significance for the top of this age.

God's Spiritual Wind

Another time Jesus addressed the wind was when Nicodemus came to Him in the night: *"And said unto him, Rabbi, we know that thou art a teacher come back from God: for no man can do these miracles that thou doest, except God be with him" (John 3:2 KJV)*. Jesus's answer to Nicodemus was, *"Except a man be born again, he cannot see the kingdom of God" (John 3:3 KJV)*. The word "see" is the Greek word *"eido."* It is derived from the Latin word *"video"* which means "to perceive with the eyes." Another meaning is "to know."

17

Nicodemus's reply was: *"How can a man be born when he is old? Can he enter the second time into his mother's womb, and be born?*

Jesus answered, Verily, verily, I say unto thee, except a man be born of water and of the Spirit, he cannot enter into the kingdom of God" (John 3:4–5 KJV).

Jesus's answer was, "Except a man is born of water and of the Spirit, he cannot enter into the kingdom of God." There is a big difference in seeing the kingdom of God and entering into the kingdom. Many who can see the kingdom will never enter because they have not been born of water or the Spirit. When we have truly been born of water, the old man has been dealt with. In his letter to the Romans, Paul explained the purpose of water baptism: *"Knowing this, that our old man is crucified with him, that the body of sin might be destroyed, that henceforth we should not serve sin" (Romans 6:6 KJV).*

When we are born of water, the old man is crucified, the body of sin is destroyed, and we are no longer a servant of sin or the old sin's nature. This is a continuous process in our life. The act of baptism is only a commitment to allow God, through the Holy Spirit, to change our lives. The apostle Peter informed us: *"Repent and be baptized every one of you in the name of Jesus Christ for the remission of sins, and ye shall receive the gift of the Holy Ghost" (Acts 2:38 KJV).*

The word "shall receive" does not mean that it is automatic. Jesus gave us further insight into receiving the Holy Spirit in our lives: *"If ye then, being evil, know how to give good gifts unto your children: how much more shall your heavenly Father give the Holy Spirit to them that ask him?" (Luke 11:13 KJV).*

If we are to receive the Holy Spirit, we must ask. It must be in our heart to allow God to change us into His image and likeness. When the Holy Spirit comes into our life, change must take place. Many today desire what they call the finished work of the cross in their lives. The finished work of the cross is the forgiveness of sin. And if that is all that is needed, there would have been no reason for the Day of Pentecost. But Pentecost did come, and the Holy Spirit was given to bring us into a place in God to be born of the Spirit. There is a difference between being baptized in the Holy Spirit and being born of the Spirit. It is only when the work of the Holy Spirit is complete, and the old man is totally destroyed with his old nature and his old way of thinking, that we will be born of the Spirit. When we are born of the Spirit, the Spirit will have complete and total control of our life. Then we, like Jesus, will say, "I only do what I see the Father doing, and I only speak what I hear the Father, saying." If we are to enter into the dominion of God, we tend to turn of water and therefore the Spirit. Many today, like Nicodemus, only have a carnal understanding of the words of Jesus. Jesus went on to explain to Nicodemus: *"That which is born of the flesh is flesh; and that which is born of the Spirit is spirit" (John 3:6 KJV).*

Many today who are claiming to be born again have not yet been born of water. They have failed to deal with the old, Adamic nature and are still servants of sin. Jesus proclaimed, "That which is born of the Spirit is a spirit." Jesus explains what happens to those who are born of the Spirit: *"The wind bloweth wherever it listeth, and thou hearest the sound thereof, but canst not tell whence it cometh, and whither it goeth: so is every one that is born of the Spirit" (John 3:8 KJV).* When we are born of the Spirit, we become like the wind because we become part of the wind. God can move us by His Spirit. The people will not know where we come from or where we are going because man will have lost all hold on our life. We will have become part of Joel's army. God gave Joel a vision of a people who have become like the wind. The four winds are God's Holy Spirit at work. And there is a twofold plan that it will accomplish and it is well said in Malachi 4:5–6 KJV, "Behold, I will send you Elijah the prophet before the coming of the great and dreadful day of the Lord: And he shall turn the heart of the fathers to the children, and the heart of the children to their fathers, lest I come and smite the earth with a curse." Rather like Ezekiel, a prophet God wants to reach His youngsters. With the Holy Spirit working through these prophets and those who teach God's truth today, the hearts of God's children will either turn back to Him or serve the world that is effectively serving Satan. God will also use the Holy Spirit, or four winds, to advance His plan in the end times. Like the wind, the Holy Spirit comes in suddenly and seemingly from nowhere. He whirls about the atmosphere and changes everything; the Spirit, like the wind, moves wherever He wants and is, at times, unpredictable. The four individual winds propelling from the east, west, north, and south directions are delineated within the Bible within the same manner as an individual's observer would describe even these days. We get a thought of the strength of those winds, the weather phenomena related to them, and their effects. However, the phrases "four winds," "four winds of the earth," or "four winds of heaven" are used in the Bible in a very different manner. The four winds are remarked within the context of extraordinary events or things as expected by prophets, created well-known to pick out persons by God within the variety of visions, or revealed by Jesus himself to His disciples. There is a third role that the four winds are going to be enjoying within the last times. John, in his vision, saw four angels standing at the four corners of the planet, holding back the four winds of the planet to stop any wind from propelling on the land or on the sea or on any tree. This would amount to a circulation pattern of the atmosphere in which there are no highs or lows or whatever, or an atmosphere of infinite calm. So now facing what is taking place in the world today, we must recognize it as no chance event, no haphazard or fortuitous occurrence, not the blind blows of fate, but the working out of the events which are coming. We must recognize that behind these events, there is power, spiritual power, and spiritual force. For despite the agony and also the unhappiness that we tend to, in our visual impairment, feel, there is the wind of the Spirit sweeping over the earth, rearranging, remaking, reshaping. And the agonies and sorrows that come, come from us—blind humans who will not enter into nature's majestic processes, helping her, but instead oppose her, and in opposing her, we suffer.

The wind of the Spirit that's propelling over the planet, tumultuous, cold, and biting as it seems to our sensitive lives, is nevertheless the wind of the Spirit, and it will blow away the fogs and illusions, and men, once more, at last, can see peace, heavenly peace, and prosperity and self-respect. It is well to remember that, while our hearts may ache and the man is inhuman whose heart today does not ache over what our brothers in humanity are enduring everywhere, behind the suffering, there's learning; behind and on the far side of these events, there's a dawn. Let us as individuals, not merely as theosophists, do our part in helping bring the new day, when violence will be seen for the folly that it is, and the reign of justice and reason and fellow feeling will be with us and around us. If not, we tend to have a repetition—or worse—of what we are now passing through, and after that, another recurrence still worse than the former, and so on, to the remains of our civilization until our civilized society will vanish in flame and blood. The tragedy of society is that it has lost its trust in an abiding spiritual power in this world of ours, and reason has lost its seat. Thus, the entire universe of ours is but an appearance, an outer shell, a physical body manifesting the tremendous forces at work on the other side of the veil of nature; and no man, no demigod, or god can offend or oppose these powers with impunity. The laws and rules of this world and, sooner or later, the gods will descend from their mighty seats. Let us see that they come to us as envoys of happiness and peace rather than with the flaming swords, avenging overthrown innocence.

Our Christian Life and Spiritual Warfare: Our Daily Challenges

Life is a battle and as Christians, we are going to face some battle or the other and we must be aware that the last days' operation of sin is increasing on a daily basis, and the host of hell has lost their wicked spirit to fight their last battle in the world. As Christians, we should be aware that we are not fighting for victory, but we are fighting from victory for our victory has already been won more than 2000 years ago. To be a heaven-bound Christian is a battle because it takes forces for people to get into the kingdom and to advance the kingdom.

Spiritual warfare is a battle fought in the supernatural. It is a conflict between the realms of the spiritual existence—the kingdom of God—and the kingdom of darkness. Spiritual warfare is fought mainly in the spiritual realm, but most of its impacts is felt in the physical realm. As beings on this planet, we are in one way involved in one battle or the other, whether be it good or bad. Spiritual warfare is real because the forces of darkness (hell) exist. They are not just a mere story or fables. As Christians, we are in the battle with unseen forces and enemies. There is spiritual warfare against the believers.

> *"For we wrestle not against flesh and blood, but against principalities, against powers, against the rulers of the darkness of this world, against spiritual wickedness in high places." (Ephesians 6:12 KJV)*

The enemies will fight us in a great number; they are numerous and uncountable, but the good news is that our God is greater than them all.

> *"Fear not: for they that be with us are more than they that be with them." (2 Kings 6:16 KJV)*

In fighting against the enemies, do not entertain any fear, for fear is the first attack of the enemy. God has not given unto us the spirit of bondage to fear again, but of sound mind with which to cry out to our Father. This enemy inflicts on our sorrow, pain, suffering, calamities, frustration, failure, delay, disappointment, reproach, defects, and the dislocation of our life. They prevent us from doing or achieving the will of God. They inflict on us plagues in a place or people, such as sickness, ignorance, fear, unbelief, poverty, barrenness, and so on. They kill, steal, and destroy our joy. They make people doubt and disbelieve the power of God for salvation. They do everything possible to keep people from reaching their promised land. They cause prayerlessness in the life of a Christian. They make us, as Christians, stumble from faith. They monitor Christians at their unguided hours so that they can attack them. They also cause loopholes in the life of a Christian. They make us do wrong things and seek also the control of man. They cause us to desire the things of the world more than that of God.

The Principles of Victory Over Our Enemies

Christ our Savior has already defeated the enemy for us, but all we need to do is to acknowledge His Lordship over our lives. To do so, the following factors must be considered:

You Must Be Born Again

> *"For whatsoever is born of God overcometh the world: and this is the victory that overcometh the world, even our faith. Who is he that overcometh the world, but he that believeth that Jesus is the Son of God...? We know that whosoever is born of God sinneth not; but he that is begotten of God keepeth himself, and that wicked one toucheth him not." (1 John 5:4–5, 18 KJV)*

You must be genuinely born again. Our victory is attached to our being born again; if we are born of God, we are untouchable and unconquerable because the blood of Jesus Christ runs in us and nothing can harm us.

Power of the Holy Spirit

You must be filled with the power of the Holy Spirit and be led by the spirit of the living God. Do not trust on your own power but on the power of the Lord God Almighty.

> *"Saying, Not by might, nor by power, but by my spirit, saith the Lord of hosts." (Zechariah 4:6 KJV)*

Knowledge of the Word

Having the knowledge of the Word, faith in the Word, and the right application of the Word of God are very important. Trusting in the Word of God is what should be our daily guide in that which we do. Let's not doubt what the Word says about our situation but instead, let us claim as we move on in the day to do our daily work or task.

> *"The devil will always deprive anyone that knows their right and fail to claim it. For God says, 'I honor my word than my names.'" (Psalms 132:2)*

Receive from God

Have the ability to hear and regularly receive instruction and information from the throne of Divine Grace on a daily basis. Your ability to hear and receive from God is very important for your victory through prayer, for prayer is the staff of Christians with which we walk with the Lord.

Understand and Undertake Spiritual Mapping

Understanding and undertaking spiritual mapping is very important because it helps you to trace the source and the roots of the problems that call for warfare. Spiritual mapping involves the analysis, divine revelation, and spiritual evidence in order to provide complete and exact data concerning the identity, strategies, and methods employed by spiritual forces of darkness to influence the people and the church. The children of Israel, in order for them to defeat the wall of Jericho, have to undergo spiritual mapping. They sent out spies to spy the land and see how it was. Spiritual mapping is a biblical principle for us to be able to conquer our enemies. In mapping, you should base it on God's Word and His revelation; you must conduct it according to those instructions given to you by God and you must carry it out with faith in the power of God.

24

Heavenly Resources

You must be aware of all the heavenly resources available to you and also make use of them. Do not be discouraged by the persistent attack. You must fight until you win the battle. Do not surrender nor retreat, but stay focused and win the battle. Joshua was persistent to God. He faithfully and obediently follows God's words and His instruction, and as a result of this, they were able to possess their promised land.

Why We Lose the Battle

As have discussed earlier, "life" is a battle that every one of us must fight in one way or another. We mainly face this battle because of a certain reason or another. There are some certain reasons why we face or lose this battle, and thus they would be examined bellow.

Sin

People lose battles because of what they find joy in doing, which is against the will of God, and this will make God distant Himself from them. It takes serious caution for everyone to live a victorious, happy, and successful life in this dangerous world. So, therefore, you must make yourself pure before God and before man so that your Father in heaven will faithfully and abundantly be with you in that which you do.

> *"Surely the arm of the Lord isn't too short to save, nor his ear too uninteresting to hear. But your iniquities have separated you from God..." (Isaiah 59:1–2 NIV)*

Fear

Fear is another weapon of attack from Satan and you should know that fear is the opposite of faith. Fear enslaves one into bondage. Exercising fear in warfare shows that one lacks faith in God for victory, and they lose the battle. Doubting the word of God makes one lose his position in the Lord. When fear is allowed, defeat will be the order of the day.

> *"For you did not receive a spirit of slavery to fall back into fear, but you have received the spirit of sonship" (Romans 8:15 RSV)*

Lack of Knowledge

The knowledge of the Word of God gives you the right to overcome the battle of life. When you have the knowledge of God's words in your life, the devil will not have an upper hand, but the opposite of this is defeat. Knowledge is power. With the Word of God in little David, he was able to defeat the giant Goliath.

> *"Therefore my people will go into exile for lack of understanding; those of rank will die of hunger and the common people will be parched with thirst." (Isaiah 5:13 NIV)*

Lack of Divine Direction

When you are divinely guided by God, you cannot lose any battle in life. Why David did not lose any battle is because he always inquired from God and walk on the platform of His divine direction. Failing to do this brings doom into one's life.

Lack of Faith

In life, we lose the battle because our faith is not at work. Faith calleth those which are not as if they were. Lack of faith in God weakens man's relationship with God. For you to win, you must activate your faith in Christ Jesus, and you will win every life's battle in this delicate world in Jesus name.

Weapons for the Warfare

God has already made available for us our weapons for our warfare, and as a result of this, we can rise in the spiritual power with our spiritual armor on and fight the good fight of faith. Each piece of our spiritual armor has the attributes of Christ which we have access to through our spiritual union, our relationship, our communion with Him, where we are drawing our strength from. Being clothed with the whole armor of God through our spiritual union with Christ has made us able to withstand every fiery dart of the enemy and to also stand up against every strategies and deceit of the enemy. The weapon for our spiritual warfare will be examined below.

The Girdle of Truth

As spiritual warriors, the very first spiritual armor we must put on as we face the enemy is the "girdle of truth." Our mind and spirit are the main sources of our strength. If our mind and spirit are strengthened and we have a clear understanding of the truth, then our will is set to follow after the truth and carries out our desires. Do not allow your heart to be weakened for your mind and spirit are the battlegrounds where Satan attacks—that is the reason why you should gird or clothe your mind and spirit with the truth, so as to enable you to withstand all the strategies and deceptions of the devil. Give yourself to the truth, for Jesus Christ gave Himself to the truth and succeeded in His battle against the world. It is the knowledge of the truth that you have that can free you from Satan. It can illuminate a man's mind and reveal his own sin and the righteousness that is of God. It removes the veil of darkness from a man's eyes and reveals God's plan and purpose for man. You must have the sonship identity of the living God and the truth of His word so that you can stand against Satan and his crew.

The Breastplate of Righteousness

God's righteousness given unto us is a breastplate against the arrows of divine wrath. The righteousness of God implanted in us fortifies our heart against the attack of Satan. The attack of Satan can come through sin, sickness, problem, poverty, death, delay, sorrows, pain curse, etc., but the breastplate of righteousness protects us from all this attack and put us in right standing before God. Being clothed in the breastplate of righteousness makes us be empowered by the Holy Spirit of God and give us the power to be invulnerable to the attack of the evil ones. It gives us the confidence, coverage, and strength to say no retreat and no surrender and make us be victorious in all battles.

The Preparation of the Gospel of Peace

The preparation of the gospel of peace covers the heart and mind. We must cloth our minds with the weapon which God has provided for our victory in the battle. Satan sometimes uses our peace to attack us and make us fearful in order to steal our peace away and cause us to lose focus on God and turn back from the gospel, which is the power of God for salvation. Without this peace, we are going to be weakened and unprepared to face Satan's attack. When we are clothed in God's peace, we become unconquerable to Satan.

> *"Peace I leave with you, my peace I give unto you: not as the world giveth, give I unto you. Let not your heart be troubled, neither let it be afraid." (John14:27 KJV)*

Stop permitting yourself to be agitated and disturbed, and do not permit yourself to be fearful and intimidated. Do not be cowardly and unsettled.

The peace of God is with us and through it, we can succeed in that which we do. This kind of peace can be ours if we engaged in the act of soul winning. He has given us His peace which will cast out all fear. Do not allow Satan to steal your peace. Be strong and do not be moved by the works of the devil.

The Shield of Faith

Faith is, all in all, in honor of temptation. Faith is relying on an unseen object, receiving Christ and the benefits of redemption, and so deriving grace from Him. Faith is like a shield, a defense in every way. The devil is the wicked one. The shield of faith is conquering faith that cannot lose a battle. Faith in action. You need to arm yourself with supernatural faith that can make you be invulnerable to the evil plans of the enemies. You need the shield of faith that resists and prevents all the fiery darts of Satan and even prevents its flames from spreading.

The Helmet of Salvation

Salvation must be our helmet. A good hope of salvation, scriptural expectations of victory will purify our soul and keep it from being defiled by Satan. The helmet of salvation should always be worn by us in order to defeat Satan. Wearing this helmet protects us from fatal wounds. The helmet of God protects and strengthens us from the attack of Satan against our spirit or heart and this is the hope of our salvation. Wearing the hope of salvation as a helmet will make us be immovable and invulnerable soldiers of Christ. Jesus Christ wearing this helmet of salvation is our supernatural hope of salvation. And through Him, we have hope and the hope fills our heart with peace and joy in the world.

The Sword of the Spirit

The sword of the spirit is the Word of God that subdue and mortify every evil desire and blasphemous attitudes or thoughts as they spring up. As you receive the Word into your heart, the Holy Spirit speaks through it, cut through and penetrates into the deep parts of the heart, and exposes the seed of sin that is there. It cuts and removes sinful thoughts that are hidden in your heart, such as lusts of the flesh, covetousness, pride, etc. As an end-time army in the kingdom of God, you must pick up the sword of the spirit of God, let the Holy Spirit of God work in your life to destroy the root of sin and cut them away. This can only be achieved by constant studying of the Word of God, by living and applying life in the sight of God. Be obedient to it, that is where you can draw strength and power to walk in victory and you will be invulnerable to Satan and his will. Be prayerful.

> *"For the word of God is quick and powerful, and sharper than any twoedged sword, piercing even to the dividing asunder of soul and spirit, and of the joints and marrow, and is a discerner of the thoughts and intents of the heart. Neither is there any creature that is not manifest in his sight: but all things are naked and opened unto the eyes of him with whom we have to do." (Hebrew 4:12–13 KJV)*

Chapter 2

The East Wind: The Destructive Wind

The east wind, also called the destructive wind, is a wind that disseminates evil occurrences. The easterly is that the wind of judgment which will blow before the New Day. The east wind was described in the Bible as a very strong, hot, and dry wind.

> *"And behold, seven thin ears and blasted with the east wind sprung up after them...*
>
> *And, behold, seven ears, withered thin, and blasted with the east wind, sprung up after them...*
>
> *And the seven thin and ill favored kine that came up after them are seven years; and the seven empty ears blasted with the east wind shall be seven years of famine." (Genesis 41:6, 23, 27 KJV)*

The Bible verses above talk about the story of the pharaoh when he had a dream. The east wind in this Bible verse represents seven years of famine that the Egyptian would face. It represents the years of great loss both in livestock and farm produces. It also represents the year of great damage. That's how strong and destructive the east wind is. The Book of Ezekiel also talks about the strong nature of the east wind:

> *"Yea, behold, being planted, shall it prosper? Shall it not utterly wither, when the east wind toucheth it? It shall wither in the furrows where it grew." (Ezekiel 17:10 KJV)*
>
> *"But she was plucked up in fury, she was cast down to the ground, and the east wind dried up her fruit: her strong rods were broken and withered; the fire consumed them." (Ezekiel 19:12 KJV)*

Nothing good comes off the east wind. The east wind is an unmoving mountain. A mountain of sorrow, pain, anguish, delay, reproach, regret, suffering, and hardship. In the Bible, the east wind was a fierce wind:

> *"By warfare and exile you contend with her—with his fierce blast he drives her out, as on the day the east wind blow." (Isaiah 27:8 NIV)*

It was a wind that damaged ships on the high seas:

> *"You destroyed them just like ships of Tarshish shattered by an east wind." (Psalm 48:7 NIV)*

The East wind can scatter and sweep out people:

> *"The east wind carries him off, and he is gone; it sweeps him out of his place." (Job 27:21 NIV)*

In the Book of Exodus, God used the east wind to destroy the people of Egypt. He (God) used the east wind to bring in swarms of locusts. Everything that survived during that period was completely destroyed and damaged by the east wind:

> *"And Moses stretched forth his rod over the land of Egypt, and the Lord brought an east wind upon the land all that day, and all the night; and when it was morning, the east wind brought the locusts.*
>
> *And the locust went up over all the land of Egypt, and rested in all the coasts of Egypt: very grievous they; before them there were no such locusts as they, neither after them shall be such.*
>
> *For they covered the face of the whole earth, so that the land was darkened; and they did eat every herb of the land, all of the fruit of the trees which the hail had left: and there remained not any green thing in the trees, or within the herbs…" (Exodus 10:13–15 KJV)*

The east wind is very destructive in nature. It destroys everything that it comes in contact with, thereby living no room for restoration. This strong and mighty wind also played a major role during the Israelite hardship in the land of Egypt, in the parting of the Red Sea when Moses led the children of Israelite out of Egypt. God Almighty used the east wind to drive back the sea, turn it into dry land, and divide the water so as to let the children of Israel pass through the dry land:

> *"Then Moses stretched out his hand over the se, and the Lord drove the sea back with a strong east wind. It blew all night and turned the sea into dry land. The water was divided." (Exodus 14:21 GNT)*

In the Book of Hosea, Hosea speaks of how an east wind will come from the Lord, blowing in from the desert; how the spring will fail; how the well will dry up; and how the storehouse will be destroyed or raid of all its treasures:

> *"Even though he thrives among his brothers. An east wind from the Lord will come, blowing in from the desert; his spring will fail and his well dry up. His storehouse will be plundered of all its treasures." (Hosea 13:15 NIV)*

The east wind also blew off the life of Jonah when he became distraught that God did not keep His word as He has promised to destroy the people of Nineveh:

> *"And it came to pass, when the sun did arise, that God prepared a vehement east wind; and the sun beat upon the head of Jonah, that he fainted and wished in himself to die, and said, It is better for me to die than to live." (Jonah 4:8 KJV)*

The east wind, which is also called *"sirocco" (from Arabic "šalūq" = "east")* is the *"scorching wind" (James 1:11)* from the desert. It is a hot, gusty wind laden with sand and dust. During this wind, it is customary for the people to close up the houses tightly to keep out the dust and heat. The heat and condition wither all vegetation *(Genesis 41:6)*. Fortunately, the wind rarely lasts for over three days at a time. East wind is the destructive "wind of the wilderness" *(Job 1:19; Jeremiah 4:11, 13:24)*.

It can be seen in the scriptures that *"Yahweh caused the sea to go back by a strong east wind all the night" (Exodus 14:21 WEB)* for the children of Israel to pass *(Isaiah 27:8)*. The strength of the wind makes it dangerous for ships at sea: *"Thou breakest the ships of Tarshish with an east wind" (Psalm 48:7)*. Euroaquilo or Euroclydon (Acts 27:14), which caused Paul's shipwreck, was an east wind that was especially dangerous in that region.

The use of east wind is shown in the scriptures with many illustrations and scriptural verses:

(1.) **Power of God:** *"He caused the east wind to blow in the heavens; and by his power he guided the south wind" (Psalms 78:26, 1 Kings 19:11; Job 27:21; 38:24; Psalms 107:25, 135:7, 147:18, 148:8; Proverbs 30:4; Jeremiah 10:13; Hosea 4:19; Luke 8:25).*

(2.) **Scattering and destruction:** *"A stormy wind shall rend it" (Ezekiel 13:11; compare 5:2; 12:14; 17:21; Hosea 4:19; 8:7; Jeremiah 49:36; Matthew 7:25).*

(3.) **Confusion:** *"tossed to and fro and carried about with every wind of doctrine" (Ephesians 4:14; compare Proverbs 27:16; Ecclesiastes 1:6; John 3:8; James 1:6).*

(4.) **Various movement:** *"toward the four winds of heaven" (Daniel 11:4; compare 8:8; Zechariah 2:6; Matthew 24:31; Mark 13:27).*

(5.) **Nothingness:** *"Molten pictures are wind" (Isaiah 41:29; compare Jeremiah 5:13).*

The east wind is very strong, hot, and dry. *Genesis 41:6, 41:23–27* shows how the heads of grain got withered by the scorching east wind. *Ezekiel (17:10, 19:12)* shows how a strong, tall vine was uprooted and stripped of its fruit by the dry east wind. The east wind is very fierce *(Isaiah 27:8; Job 38:24)*, it destroys *(Psalm 48:7; Ezekiel 27:26)*, scatters, and sweep out *(Job 15:2, 27:21; Jonah 4:8; Jeremiah 18:17)*. The east wind was used by God to part the waters of the Red Sea. These reveal the power of the east wand, how it can affect lives negatively, especially from the spiritual perspective. The easterly comes with crisis or tragedy, brings destruction, famine, empties churches, pockets, etc. Dispersion is likened to wind and scattering to a whirlwind, which is said to be of evil, then they who are regenerate shall rejoice in Jehovah.

> *"For lo, the kings were assembled, they passed by together. They saw it, then and so they marvelled; they were troubled, and hasted away. Fear took hold upon them there, and pain, as of a woman in travail. Thou breakest the ships of Tarshish with an east wind."* *(Psalm 48:4–7 KJV)*.

The terror and confusion were caused by an east wind; the description from what passes in the world of spirits, which is in the internal sense of the Word. It is used in the Book of Jeremiah to make the land desolate: *"I will scatter them as with an east wind before the enemy; I will shew them the back, and not the face, in the day of their calamity."* *(Jeremiah 18:17 KJV)*.

The east wind also dried up the Red Sea so that the sons of Israel might pass over, as described in Exodus: *"Jehovah caused the sea to go [back] by a strong east wind all the night, and made the sea dry land, and the waters were divided"* *(Exodus 14:21 ASV)*. The importance of the waters of the Red Sea was similar to the waters of the flood in the present passage, as seen from the fact that the Egyptians (represented by the wicked) were drowned therein, while the sons of Israel (represented by the regenerate) passed over. The Red Sea, the same as the flood, represented damnation and temptation; and thus, by the east wind, signifies the dissipation of the waters, of the evils of damnation, or of temptation. "And the Lord shall utterly destroy the tongue of the Egyptian sea; and with his mighty wind shall he shake his hand over the river, and shall smite it in the seven streams, and make them go over dryshod. And there shall be an highway for the remnant of his people, which shall be left, from Assyria; like as it was to Israel in the day that he came up out of the land of Egypt" (Isaiah11:15–16). Ezekiel refers to the "east wind" additionally as "fire." This is the precise combination that we have a tendency to be perceptive within the wildfires happening straight away in Israel.

The Holy Scriptures that talks about the east wind:

"Should a wise man utter vain knowledge, and fill his belly with the east wind?" (Job 15:2 KJV)

"The east wind carrieth him away, and he departeth: and as a storm hurleth him out of his place." (Job 27:21 KJV)

"He caused an east wind to blow in the heaven [see Heavens Below, Heavens Above]*: and by his power, he brought within the south wind." (Psalm 78:26 KJV)*

"In measure, when it shooteth forth, thou wilt debate with it: he stayeth his rough wind in the day of the east wind." (Isaiah 27:8 KJV)

"To make their land desolate, and a perpetual hissing; every one that passeth thereby shall be astonished, and wag his head. I will scatter them as with an east wind before the enemy; I will shew them the back, and not the face, in the day of their calamity." (Jeremiah 18:16–17 KJV)

"But she was plucked up in fury, she was cast down to the ground, and the east wind dried up her fruit: her strong rods were broken and withered; the fire consumed them." (Ezekiel 19:12 KJV)

> *"I will ransom them from the power of the grave* [see through the gates of hell]*; I will redeem them from death: O death, I will be thy plagues; O grave, I will be thy destruction: repentance shall be hid from mine eyes. Though he be fruitful among his brethren, an east wind shall come, the wind of the LORD shall come up from the wilderness area, and his spring shall become dry, and his fountain shall be dried up: he shall spoil the treasure of all pleasant vessels."* (Hosea 13:14–15 KJV)

> *"And it came to pass, when the sun did arise, that God prepared a vehement east wind; and the sun beat upon the head of Jonah* [see also "The Prophets: Jonah"]*, that he fainted, and wished in himself to die, and said, It is better for me to die than to live."* (Jonah 4:8 KJV)

> *"They shall come all for violence: their faces shall sup up because the east wind, and that they shall gather the captivity as the sand."* (Habakkuk 1:9 KJV)

East wind from the desert and wilderness of Sinai were concerned within the far-famed apocalyptic dreams that were properly taken, as made possible by the Lord, by Joseph (while he was still a falsely accused prisoner; see "Joseph, Prime Minister of Egypt").

The Nile Delta

> *And he slept and dreamed the second time: and, behold, seven ears of corn came up upon one stalk, rank and good. And, behold, seven thin ears and blasted with the east wind sprung up after them. And the seven thin ears devoured the seven rank and full ears. And Pharaoh awoke, and, behold, it was a dream."* (Genesis 41:5–7 KJV)

The Lord (Jesus Christ) says in 1 Corinthians 10:1–4 KJV, "Moreover, brethren, I would not that ye should be ignorant, how that all our fathers were under the cloud, and all passed through the sea; and were all baptized unto Moses within the cloud and in the sea; and did all eat the same spiritual meat; and did all drink the same spiritual drink: for they drank of the spiritual Rock that followed them: and that Rock was Christ." "Before Abraham Was, I AM," he used the east wind to deliver the locusts as one of the plagues upon Egypt before the Exodus.

> *"And the locust went up over all the land of Egypt, and rested in all the coasts of Egypt: very grievous were they; before them there were no such locusts as they, neither after them shall be such. For they covered the face of the whole earth, so that the land was darkened; and they did eat every herb of the land, and all the fruit of the trees that the hail had left: and there remained not any green thing in the trees, or in the herbs of the field, through all the land of Egypt."*
> *(Exodus 10:14–15 KJV)*

The parting of the sea was done by an east wind that blew all night ("the Lord caused the ocean to travel back by a powerful east wind all that night, and made the sea dry land"), leaving a "wall" (i.e. a barrier; see "The Walls of Water") of water on either side of the path made dry through the ocean (see "Why Through the Sea?").

Parting of the Sea

> *"But the children of Israel walked upon dry land in the midst of the sea; and the waters were a wall unto them on their right hand, and on their left. Thus the LORD saved Israel that out of the hand of the Egyptians; and Israel saw the Egyptians dead upon the sea shore. And Israel saw that great work which the LORD did upon the Egyptians: and the people*

feared the LORD, and believed the LORD, and his servant Moses." (Exodus 14:29–31 KJV)

What Is the Importance of "East Wind" in the Bible?

"Though he may flourish among his brothers, the east wind, the wind of the Lord, shall come, rising from the wilderness, and his fountain shall dry up; his spring shall be parched; it shall strip his treasury of each precious thing." (Hosea 13:15 KJV)

The "east wind" here refers to Shalmaneser V, who was one of the kings of Assyria and who came from the east. The verse goes on to say "the wind of the LORD..."—which means that this was an event ordained and allowed by Him as part of His providence. Naturally, the wind that came from the east side was very strong and used to blast all vegetation, so king Shalmaneser V is thus compared, as he came to destroy Israel in a vehement manner. This attribution of the east wind to King Shalmaneser V is figurative, and the language is very common in the Holy Scriptures. The winds that come to Palestine from the east come from the desert. This indicates that it is hot *(Jeremiah 4:11)*. The plague of locusts on Egypt came from the east wind *(Exodus 10:13)*. *In Exodus 14:21*, the east wind dried the sea for the crossing of the Israelites. Genesis 41:6—the east wind blasted ears of corn. *Psalm 48:7*—broken ships. *Ezekiel 27:26; Ezekiel 17:10*—withered plants. *Hosea 13:15*—dried fountains. *Jonah 4:8*—Jonah was smitten. The east wind indicates a judgment from God *(Isaiah 27:8; Jeremiah 18:17)*. Wind is seen as a vector quantity having both speed and direction. Here, by convention, wind or easterly wind means one that's blowing from the east, and so on.

The Bible shows several references to the power of the wind, its variability, and its destructive potential. Only the four basic directions—east, west, north, and south—are talked about. Out of the four winds of the Bible, the east wind is mostly mentioned and generally described as a very strong, hot, and dry wind. Genesis 41:6, 41:23, 41:27 talk of the heads of grain that sprouted and then got withered by the scorching east wind. The Book of Ezekiel verses 17:10, 19:12 tell how the strong and tall vine was uprooted and got completely withered and stripped of its fruit by the dry east wind. The east wind in the Bible is also a fierce wind *(Isaiah 27:8; Job 38:24)*, destroy ships on the high seas *(Psalm 48:7; Ezekiel 27:26)*, scatter and sweep out people *(Job 15:2, 27:21; Jonah 4:8; Jeremiah 18:17)*. The Book of Exodus shows how God brought in ten different forms of plagues over Egypt. The seventh plague was the plague of hail, followed by the eighth plague which was the plague of locusts *(Exodus 10:13)*. The sequence was such the huge hailstorms had already rendered the land wet. The next morning, God used the wind to herald a swarm of locusts, which was found in the wet, sandy soil—an ideal environment to lay eggs and breed in huge numbers. Whatever had survived the hail was completely devoured by the locusts. God changed the direction of the wind the following day to a very strong west wind. It trapped the locusts and carried them into the Red Sea, and not a locust was left anywhere in Egypt *(Exodus 10:19)*. The strong and dry east wind played an important role in the parting of the waters of the Red Sea that enabled the Israelites to cross it. God used the sturdy wind to drive the ocean back, turn it into dry land, and divide the waters *(Exodus 14:21)*. The sheer power of the wind that created all this potential was remembered for long *(Psalm 78:26)*. In the Book of Hosea, there is a warning for those who feed on the wind, pursues the east wind all day, and multiplies lies and violence *(12:1)*. An east wind from the Lord will come, blowing in from the desert; his spring will fail and his well dry up. His depository are pillaged of all its treasures *(Hosea 13:15)*. Hosea speaks of the deeds of evildoers in these words *(8:7):* "They sow the wind and reap the windstorm." God's Word speaks of the east wind more than any of the other winds; it is referred to twenty-one times. When God was going to bring judgment upon Egypt to deliver His people, He used the east wind twice. The first time:

> *"And Moses stretched forth his rod over the land of Egypt, and the Lord brought an east wind upon the land all that day, and all that night; and when it was morning, the east wind brought the locusts."*
> *(Exodus 10:13 KJV)*

Locusts are always a sign of destruction. Nothing lives in the path of the locust. God used the east wind to bring judgment upon all vegetation Egypt depended on to sustain life. God's judgment is always swift and complete.

The second time God used the east wind to bring judgment upon Egypt:

> *"And Moses stretched out his hand over the sea; and the Lord caused the sea to go back by a strong east wind all that night, and made the sea dry land, and the waters were divided." (Exodus 14:21 KJV)*

The east wind divided the Red Sea. The dividing of the Red Sea brought retrieval to God's folks. The east wind allowed God's people to cross over on dry ground, but to the Egyptian Army, the East Wind meant total annihilation. God's people were completely delivered from any threat of the pharaoh's army. The east wind always blows from the direction of the new day. For Egypt, it was the end. All their vegetation was gone—their crops, their livestock, all trees. Death was in every house. Their army and all their young men were destroyed.

To Israel, it was the beginning of a new day. They were released from their slavery. Taskmasters no longer had dominion in their lives. They were set free to worship their god and to plan their own future. They were free to act upon the promises of God, free to enter the land flowing with milk and honey. We, too, look forward to the time when God will set His people free from all the bondage of the governmental taskmasters. God is about to lead His people into His new day, the glorious kingdom of God. God declares His east wind in many ways. The psalmist wrote:

> *"Thou breakest the ships of Tarshish with an east wind." (Psalm 48:7 KJV)*

The word *"Tarshish"* means "she will bring poverty, or she will scatter." Tarshish also means "a time of testing or a place of heat." When God sends His East Wind upon the earth, it will be a time of testing and breaking. Those who will not be broken (humbled), now

41

will be broken when the angels release the four winds to blow upon the earth.

Ephraim Feedeth on the Wind

God foretold the wind of judgment He would bring upon the tribes of Ephraim and Dan. Jeroboam had set up his golden calves in these two tribes. Because of this, God totally destroyed the tribes of Ephraim and Dan. They do not appear in the spiritual tribes of Revelation 7. Neither of these tribes will be part of the one hundred and forty-four thousand. God did not reveal what happened to Dan, but the prophet Hosea foretold the fate of Ephraim:

> *"Ephraim feedeth on wind, and followeth after the east wind: he daily increaseth lies and desolation; and they do make a covenant with the Assyrians, and oil is carried into Egypt." (Hosea 12:1 KJV)*

The east wind is the wind of the Lord. The wind of the Lord came upon Ephraim because he daily increased lying. Ephraim not only lied to others, but he also lied to himself. Many today, like Ephraim, tell themselves they are the chosen of God, and all they have to do is offer an innocent animal (ask forgiveness) and they will be restored in the grace of God. Many today, like Ephraim, have overlooked the scriptures that state:

> *"Thou shalt have no other gods before me."*
> *(Exodus 20:3 KJV)*

When we have made gods unto ourselves, we invoke the east wind of God's wrath in our lives. Ephraim also increased desolation in his life. The word "desolation" means "havoc, destruction, ruin, and violence." Many wonder why there are so many problems in their lives. It is because, like Ephraim, they have allowed false gods to be set up in their lives. Therefore, it is because of this that God's judgment winds are blowing, not to destroy them, but to bring them to true repentance. Ephraim made a covenant with Assyria. The word "Assyria" means "to step up in society." Those who have made a covenant with Assyria have come into agreement with the world. They desire the things of the world more than the things of God. There is no separation in their life. They are in agreement with the heathen. They have been taught they have a right to demand from God all the things the heathens possess and trust in. Not only did Ephraim come into agreement with Assyria, but they also carried their oil into Egypt. They have taken their anointing back into the world. The fruit of the spirit they possess are only for show, displayed before the world to show how great their anointing is before God. The fruit of the spirit in their lives have become almost nonexistent. There is no evidence of love. Joy is displayed as happiness only when they have acquired some new toy. Their peace is only evident when there is no adversity. This peace is easily lost with the slightest problem. Long suffering is not even considered in their walk with God. These have taken their fruit and their anointing to the world and they are feeding on the wind. Hosea continued his revelation of God's judgment upon Ephraim:

"Though he be fruitful among his brethren, an east wind shall come, the wind of the Lord shall come up from the wilderness, and his spring shall become dry, and his fountain shall be dried up: he shall spoil the treasure of all pleasant vessels." (Hosea 13:15 KJV)

Ephraim's springs have dried up. The springs of water in our life are the anointed Word of God. When our springs dry up, the Word becomes meaningless, just a dry morsel. This is when God spoils or robs the treasures He has hidden in His Word, and they fall away. Hosea continued:

"For Israel slideth back as a backsliding heifer: now the Lord will feed them as a in a large place. Ephraim is joined to idols: let him alone." (Hosea 4:16–17 KJV)

God called Israel a backsliding heifer, and Ephraim had joined himself to idols. God directed, "Let him alone." Many today, like

Ephraim, are following after the east wind, but their way of life demands the judgment of God. There will be weeping, wailing, and gnashing of teeth when the wind of the Lord blows upon the earth. The angels are holding back the east wind. When God releases the east wind upon the earth, His judgment will be released in all its fury upon all things that are unclean and defiled in the sight of God.

The Vehement East Wind in Nineveh

The prophet Jonah was sent to Nineveh to prophesy that if they did not repent, God was going to totally destroy Nineveh and all that was in it. The king of Nineveh declared a fast and the whole city repented, and God's hand of judgment has stayed. The prophet Jonah became distraught because he felt God had not kept His word, so Jonah went out of the city and was angry with the Lord:

> *"And it came to pass once the sun did arise, that God prepared a vehement east wind; and the sun beat upon the head of Jonah, that he fainted, and wished in himself to die, and said, It is better for me to die than to live." (Jonah 4:8 KJV)*

The wind of judgment blew upon Jonah's rebellion, and he desired to die. Jonah thought it would be better to be dead than to face the people who would consider him a false prophet. The Bible speaks of another time when man will desire death, but death will not be available to him:

> *"And there came out of the smoke locusts upon the earth: and unto them was given power, as the scorpions of the earth have power...*
> *And to them, it was given that they should not kill them, but that they should be tormented five months: and their torment was as the torment of a scorpion, when he striketh a man. And in those days shall men seek death,*

and shall not find it; and shall desire to die, and death shall flee from them." (Revelation 9:3, 5–6 KJV)

When God releases the east wind, His judgment will be released upon all the earth in the form of locusts, and they will torment man for five months. This torment will be such that man, like Jonah, will want to die, but death will flee from them. The east wind is for those who will not hear God's voice, nor heed His words while it is yet day time. For when the night comes they will be in the midst of the east wind with no place of escape.

Job's East Wind

When Job's three friends came to him in his time of testing, Eliphaz related to Job:

"Should a wise man utter vain knowledge, and fill his belly with the east wind?" (Job 15:2 KJV)

The word translated vainly is the Hebrew word *"ruwach"* and it means "breath or spirit." Eliphas was asking Job if a man should utter spiritual knowledge with only physical understanding. Many today are aware of the judgment of God that is about to be released upon all God's creations, yet they refuse to prepare their lives for the inevitable. God desires for them to see with spiritual understanding, yet they continue to apply His Word physically to their life instead of making the spiritual adjustments needed to be delivered from the east wind. They are only filling their bellies with the east wind of God's judgment when the four angels release the four winds of heaven.

What Is So Bad About the East Wind?

In the land of Israel, winds normally blow from the Mediterranean Sea inland in an eastward direction. This has the positive impact of delivering cool wet air (and rain throughout the winter months) to the whole country. However, the opposite can also happen. When the winds blow from the Arabian Desert region westward, the result is very unpleasant. Hot dry winds distribute a caustic blanket of dirt across the whole country. The minute grains of desert dirt kill crops and acquire into each crevice, making respiration terribly tough. The image below could be a satellite photograph showing a vast cloud of dirt from the peninsula desert (bottom) headed for Israel (top). The prophet Hosea predicts that because of the idolatry and wickedness of the individuals of Israel, God will punish them. This punishment will be unexpected and quick, similar to the way in which the east wind suddenly covers the entire land of Israel with dust, drying up natural sources of water. Although he may flourish among rushes, the east wind shall come, a blast from the Lord, rising from the wilderness; and his fountain shall dry up, his spring shall be parched. It shall strip his treasury of each precious factor. Notice, however, the prophet clearly notes that this sort of damaging wind comes from the "wilderness" that is the Arabian Desert to the east of the land of Israel *(Hosea 13:15)*. In the passage, the prophet Ezekiel laments the destruction of the kingdom of Judah at the hands of Babylon by alluding to a vineyard attacked by the east wind:

> *"Your mother was like a vine in your vineyard planted by the water; it was fruitful and full of branches because of abundant water. Its branches were strong, fit for a ruler's scepter. It towered high above the thick foliage, conspicuous for its height and for its many branches. But it was uprooted in fury and thrown to the ground. The east wind made it shrivel, it was stripped of its fruit; its strong branches withered and fire consumed them." (Ezekiel 19:10–12 NIV).*

Benefits of the East Wind

1. It makes a way for us in the wilderness of life. This is evident in the parting of the Red Sea:

    "And Moses stretched his hand over the sea, and the Lord caused the sea to go back by a strong east wind all that night, and made the sea dry land, and the waters were divided." (Exodus 14:21 KJV)

2. Through this wind, the wicked shall receive their judgment.

Sinners in the Hand of an Angry God

God is going to rain down His vengeance upon the wicked ones. God is going to make His judgment shine upon every one of their sins. God's anger is going to be released upon those who brought forth bitter and poisonous fruits. God is going to expose them to destruction. They are going to fall and they will fail. The day is coming when everyone will have to stand face to face with Jesus Christ to answer for himself. He will not be able to take comfort in being one among many. He will see no other. There will be no place to hide. Earth and heaven flee before the face of Him that sitteth on the throne. Seeing nothing but Him, the sinner has to stand in the light, naked and alone, to talk with his Redeemer. He may urge his excuses then, and plead his cause if he will, but he will be speechless. He has slighted divine love, and he is without excuse. He hears his sentence, and he feels that God is just. King Hezekiah in the Scriptures was the king of Judah before the fall of Judah. He reigned in the turbulent times in Judah like our time. He idolized God and was an awfully humble leader. He elevated the social, political, and religious lifetime of the individuals. Even once, God told Isaiah, the prophet, to inform him he ought to set his house, so as a result of what he was planning to take him and he would die. He challenged God with these words. But his son, King Manasseh, was not so. All the good work his father did, he reversed and attained the name "The king who created Judah's sin." Before the autumn of Judah, King Hezekiah had gotten rid of all the worship the individuals of Judah participated in: destroyed Semitic deity worship, cleaned the temple, led the individuals to a religious revival, renovated and rebuilt the infrastructure of Judah and Jerusalem; but his son, King Manasseh, will undo them. King Manasseh did the following:

- He did evil and built the high places his father demolished.
- He created altars for Baal and did not worship God.
- Created Asherah poles and bowed to star-like hosts.
- Engineered altars and carven pictures to be worshiped within the temple of the Lord wherever God said: "in the temple and Jerusalem, is the city in Judah He has chosen for his name to remain forever."
- He sacrificed his son in the fire in the valley of Ben Hinnom.
- He practiced sorcery, divination, witchcraft.
- He consulted medium, spirits

The Lord spoke to Manasseh and his individuals, but they paid no attention. So the Lord brought against them the army commander of Assyria who took Manasseh prisoner, put a hook on his nose, bound him with a bronze shackle, and took him to Babylon. God is so good, so merciful, and so compassionate. It has never been the need of God to destroy humans He created.

The wrath of God is like nice water that's dammed for the current, they increase more and more, rise higher and higher till an outlet is given, and the longer the stream is stopped, the more rapid and mighty its course, when once it is let loose. It is true that judgment against your evil works has not been dead as yet, the flood of God's vengeance have been withheld, our guilt in the meantime is constantly increasing and we are everyday treasuring up more wrath. If God ought to solely withdraw His hand from the floodgate, it would immediately fly open, and the fiery floods of the fierceness and wrath of God would rush forth with inconceivable fury and would come upon us with omnipotent power. The bow of God's wrath is bent and the arrow is made ready on the string, and justice bends the arrows at our heart and strains the bow, and it is nothing, however, it is the mere pleasure of God and that of an angry God. We should consider the fearful danger we are in. It is an excellent chamber of wrath, a wide and bottomless pit, full of the fire of wrath.

We All Have Sinned

Sin is deliberate disobedience to the laws, rules, and regulations of God. We have all sinned. There is nobody on the planet who never sins. You need not wait on God to do something. He has already done what needs to be done. He gave His only Son to die in our place because only a perfect and sinless sacrifice could be offered to pay for our misdeeds. Justice has been satisfied, and we can go free through believing in Jesus Christ and by entering an intimate relationship with God through Him. God's Word says our sin will find us out. Sin brings a curse and obedience brings blessing. It may appear for a season that a person is getting by with their sin; their life seems to be as good as anyone else's, but in the end, there will always be evidence of the choices they have made. Choosing a life of sin rather than a life of obedience to God makes us experience misery in our souls. Man is more than a body made of flesh and bones. He is a spirit and he has a soul which is comprised of mind, will, and emotions. Sinners suffer in their mind. They are filled with mental anguish, and no matter what they do or possess, there is nothing that completely satisfies them, making them suffer emotionally. Since they have chosen to run their own lives, they become frustrated and angry when things do not go their way. They know nothing of the way of faith. Trusting God's power is greater than themselves is incomprehensible to them. They never enter rest in their souls as a result of one might solely enter the remainder of God through the basic cognitive process in Him.

Conclusion

In conclusion, the east wind is a wind of disaster, a wind of discomfort, a judgmental wind that God is going to use to judge His people here on earth. If you are experiencing this wind, all you need to do is to trace your way back to your Creator by taking the following steps:

1. Come plain before Him.
2. Ask Him to forgive you of all your wrongdoings.
3. Ask Him to fill your life once again.
4. Totally surrender all yourself to Him.
5. Ask Him to lead you in the way that is right.
6. Ask Him to direct and guide you in your daily living.

Prayer Tip

Father, I personally ask you to blow your wind upon me, upon your church, and upon the mission organizations I support, so they will all be "moved" by the Spirit and supernaturally empowered to do the work of the ministry.

Chapter 3

The North Wind: The Wind of Reversal

The north wind, also known as the reversal wind, is the direction of God's throne. It is the wind of power, majesty, and authority. The north wind blew from God's throne, bringing to us our deliverance. Though we sin against God, thereby causing Him (God) to rain His judgment upon us (east wind), but still, He delivers (north wind) us from judgment and gives unto us peace of mind. As judgment comes from God, so does deliverance. The Israelite sinned against God, which in turn paved way for God's judgment upon them. But God, in His infinite mercy, after hearing their cry and hard labor they are faced in Egypt, also delivered them from the hands of the Egyptian.

"So they put slave masters over them to oppress them with forced labor, and they built Pithom and Rameses as store cities for Pharaoh." (Exodus 1:11 NIV)

"Therefore, say to the Israelites, 'I am the Lord, and I will bring you out from under the yoke of the Egyptians. I will free you from being slaves to them, and I will redeem you with an outstretched arm and with mighty acts of judgment.'" (Exodus 6:6 NIV)

Our carnality and wicked nature is the true reason why we do not partake of the benefits that the north wind brings. The north wind comes with a lot of benefits which may include:

1. **Deliverance:** Been totally set free or set loose from the problems or strong situation, which is beyond your powers or problems that you are facing.
2. **Recovery:** The regaining act or repossessing act of that which belongs to you that was forcefully taken away from you or that was deprived of you.

51

3. **Freedom:** The act of someone being liberated from the bondage he or she is facing, which is causing such individual pain or sorrow.
4. **Blessings:** The undeserved breakthrough, promotion, lifting, success that we enjoy.

The north wind brings deliverance to God's people. Let's take a look at the man at the pool of Bethesda. The man was afflicted with a certain sickness for a good thirty-eight years. The east wind blew upon the man, but in a twinkling of an eye, the man was made whole by Jesus when he experienced the peaceful north wind of deliverance.

> *"Now a certain man was there who had an infirmity thirty-eight years. When Jesus saw him lying there, and knew that he already had been in that condition for a long time, He said to him, 'Do you want to be made well?' The sick man answered Him, 'Sir, I have no man to put me into the pool when the water is stirred up; but while I am coming, another steps down before me.'*
>
> *Jesus said to him, 'Rise, take up your bed and walk.' And immediately the man was made well, took up his bed and walked." (John 5:5–9 NKJV)*

When the north wind blew upon us as God's people, we are going to partake of His pleasant fruits—the fruit of the spirit. This fruit will be manifested in the flesh by and through the spirit. The north wind could also be described as a wind of redemption (salvation from sin) through grace, so that we can be called the sons of God.

> *"For by grace you have been saved through faith, and that not of yourselves; it is the gift of God, not of works, that no one would boast." (Ephesians 2:8–9 HNV)*

"For he hath made him to be sin for us, who knew no sin; that we might be made the righteousness of God in him." (2 Corinthians 5:21 KJV)

Even without sin, without iniquities, Jesus died for our sins. He paid the debt he did not owe. We enjoyed that grace of being called God's people. The northern is sometimes a powerful, continuous wind blowing down from the northern hills, and whereas it changes state, it continuously "drives away rain," as properly explained in *Proverbs 25:2,* yet it is a disagreeable wind and often causes headache and fever.

The north wind is the wind that brings rain *(Proverbs 25:23),* windstorm, and brilliant flashes of lightning *(Ezekiel 1:4).* The north wind brings conviction, judgment, reproving, and so on *(Job 37:22).*

"When he uttereth his voice, there is a multitude of waters in the heavens; and he causeth the vapours to ascend from the ends of the earth: he maketh lightnings with rain and bringeth forth the wind out of his treasures." (Jeremiah 51:16 KJV)

Elihu, the spirit-filled young man, told Job:

"Fair weather cometh out of the north: with God is terrible majesty." (Job 37:22 KJV)

The word "terrible" suggests "to interchange awe and reverent fear." When God's fair weather returns to the earth, we are going to stand in awe and reverence of the majesty God is going to display to His people.

Solomon Declared the North Wind

"The wind goeth toward the south, and turneth about unto the north; it whirleth about continually, and the

wind returneth again according to his circuits."
(Ecclesiastes 1:6 KJV)

The current of air blows from the throne of God, transporting retrieval. Solomon wrote that it whirleth about continually. God's deliverance and refreshment are on the earth continually. As judgment comes from God, so does deliverance. God's judgment wind will blow, but the south wind will bring the time of refreshment, and God will send deliverance by the north wind. It is only because of our wickedness and our carnal mind that we do not partake of the north and south winds in our lives. God has made it continually available to us, only we have not come into a place to receive it. Solomon spoke again of the continual whirling of the north and south winds:

"Awake, O north wind; and come, thou south; blow
upon my garden, that the spices thereof may flow out.
Let my beloved come into his garden, and eat his
pleasant fruits." (Song of Solomon 4:16 KJV)

Solomon was speaking of those who would make up God's Holy City, the Bride of Christ. He wrote, "Awake, O North Wind, come thou south, blow upon my garden." We are the garden of the Lord. In fact, He calls us His "garden of nuts."

"I went down into the garden of nuts to see the fruits of
the valley, and to see whether the vine flourished and the
pomegranates budded." (Song of Solomon 6:11 KJV)

This truly is not a derogatory statement. Nuts are the fruit or seed of trees. We are His trees of righteousness. God was speaking of checking the fruit we have produced in our lives. These are the fruit of the Spirit, and His north wind blows upon us so the spices may flow out of our lives. Spices, in the Bible, are used as sweet-smelling fragrances and also as healing balms. Paul spoke of these:

"For we are unto God a sweet savour of Christ, in them that are saved, and in them that perish." (II Corinthians 2:15 KJV)

When the wind from the north blows upon God's people, they will partake of His pleasant fruits, the fruit of the Spirit. These fruits will be manifest in the flesh by and through the Spirit. This will not be the first fruit anointing, but the double portion anointing that comes from the throne of God.

Benefits of the North Wind

1. It gives unto us the power and authority of the things on this earth.

    "And having called together the twelve, he gave them power and authority over all demons, and to heal diseases." (Luke 9:1 DBY)

2. Gives unto us total recovery of that which belongs to us that has been lost either due to sin or being forcibly taken away from us.

    "'But I will restore you to health and heal your wounds,' declares the Lord..." (Jeremiah 30:17 NIV)

3. It gives us total freedom from the powers oppressing our lives. It is for freedom that Christ has set America free.

    "Stand firm therefore, and do not let yourselves be burdened again by a yoke of slavery."
    (Galatians 5:17 NIV)

Moving Your Mountain: The Wind of Reversal

Moving your mountains means doing or achieving that thing that seems impossible to do or that thing that is incredibly difficult. We all have one mountain or another that need to be moved. There are several promises of God for us and every one of your heart desires is contained in this promise of God for your life. In moving your mountain, you need to take the following steps:

Believe in the biblical confession

You need to take God's words for what it is. You need to confess God's words before you do a thing and see the answer. You need to confess with your mouth that your needs are met according to God's Word. You need to confess and face those circumstances with the Word of God.

Practice faith

Have the faith in that which you do not doubt yourself or your abilities. Believe that what God says He will do for you, He will do it. God has promised you in His Word that you will enjoy and live a divine destiny. Believe in God's promise, confess God's promise, and receive God's promise. Believe those things that God says will come to pass. Receive by faith that which God says He is going to give unto you. Hold on unto Him because He's going to bring to pass that which He said.

Confess it as a corresponding action

Faith without corresponding action is dead. Believe and act on that which God said He will do. Confessing the Word is one of the ways you act on the Word. If God promised us something in his Word, you should confess that it is yours before you actually see it manifested.

Hold on to your confession

Talk in line with the Word of God so that you can receive your inheritance in Christ. God Himself backs up your confession when your claim is based on your inheritance in Christ. Believe in your heart so that your confession can be biblical. Base your faith and your confession on the Word of God and your faith will work for you. You need to know that you are going to get in life that which you believe in your heart and what you say with your mouth. The biblical principle of faith is believing in your heart and speaking your conviction with your mouth.

Put God in remembrance of His Word

When your confession is not based on the Word of God, it has no validity to it. It carries no weight in the court of Heaven. You need to put God in remembrance of His word and His word will prosper in that situation you are facing. Putting God in remembrance of His word is a way of calling the attention of God to that which He already promised us. It is of great pleasure to God when we study and meditate on His Word until it's down on the inside of us in our heart and then we bring it to His remembrance.

Talk in line with God's Word

Always talk in line with God's Word. The fact of God's Word is higher than medical facts. God's Word contains supernatural facts. What does God say in his Word concerning your healing, hold on to it. God is more than enough to meet every one of your needs, and by His great power, He can come down and change every natural facts and circumstance. His power on the scene brings health and healing. His power on the scene brings miracles and abundantly meets our needs.

Identify your mountain

Before you can speak or move a mountain, you first need to identify what mountain it is that you are facing. Find out what the mountain of hindrance is that has kept you from reaching your promise land. Sometimes, the reason why we do not receive answers to our prayer is that we never sometimes identify our problems. To identify the mountain, you also need to pray to God and ask Him to identify the source of those mountains for us. Every person has their own insurmountable mountain in life. We each have our own personalities and different mountains that have tried to hinder us spiritually from possessing our promised land. What has an effect on one person might not affect another person. What is a stumbling block to one may not be a stumbling block to others. To be able to move these mountains, you need to identify the mountain itself.

Be bold

You have to be bold in order for you to speak to your mountain. You cannot accomplish anything by meekly trying to speak to a problem that is hindering your progress. You have to speak with authority that is in the name of Jesus and also speak the Word of God against such a problem. Learn to use your authority and power to move that mountain. Move those situations with God giving authority and power that was bestowed on you.

Faith Application in Moving Your Mountain

You need faith for you to be able to move your mountain. Faith can be defined as unreserved confidence in God, in His love for me, and in His power to help me whatever comes my way in life. Faith is a choice.

> *"But where there is no faith it is impossible to please Him; for the man who draws near to God must believe that there is God and that He proves Himself a rewarder of those who earnestly try to find Him." (Hebrews 11:6 WNT)*

In moving your mountain, you need to have faith in the Word and promises of God for your life. For each and every one of us to enter and possess the richness and goodies of our promised land, we need to believe in the Word of God. We need to remind ourselves daily that we are going to receive from God and appropriately what belongs to us. Remind yourself that God has already bought and paid for your inheritance in Christ and that He's promised it to you. Then receive it for yourself and believe that God will do what He promised. You need to realize that anything that God has promised you in His Word already belongs to you. All of God blessings and benefits are part of your promised land. The devil will try to forcibly take those blessings away from you. To avoid such, you need to talk in line with God and have the faith in Him that you have already possessed those inheritances in Him. Do not be moved or do not believe any evil report of the devil concerning your inheritance in Christ Jesus. An evil report will not only hurt your faith, but it can also affect those around you. To be successful in that which God has for you, you have to say and meditate on His Word. Do not think negative about yourself. Do not doubt or disbelief yourself. Do not say "I can't." It is the promise of God to you that you can do all things through His strength that He has bestowed upon you.

"I can do all things through Christ which strengtheneth me." (Philippians 4:13 KJV)

God in His Word never wanted or wished for us that we should say "I can't" because He *can* through us. I remembered when I finished my university education and was hoping to get a good job before going for my service, others were saying they can't, I was saying I can and miraculously, God provided a good job for me. If that principle is true in nature, how much more is its truthfulness with the power of God working in our lives? With God, you can do all things. God works through our impossibilities and helps us to achieve the impossible in our life. He turns every impossibility to possibility. When God promises you something, He gives it to you. God already have every one of your problems solved if you can just trust and have faith in Him. Stop meditating on your doubts and unbelief because, if you do not stop, it can work you into frenzy. Get yourself off your problem so that you can receive from God. The Israelites did not do this. They did not guard what God has promised them; they did not keep their eyes on their goal. Instead, they murmured and complained and that got their eyes off the goal. When the ten spies told the other Israelites that it was impossible to possess the Promised Land, they came together in a committee and began to murmur and complain against Moses and Aaron. They doubted God's Word for their lives.

> *"And all the congregation lifted up their voice, and cried; and the people wept that night. And all the children of Israel murmured against Moses and against Aaron: and the whole congregation said unto them, Would God that we had died in the land of Egypt! Or would God we had died in this wilderness! And wherefore hath the LORD brought us unto this land, to fall by the sword, that our wives and our children should be a prey? Were it not better for us to return into Egypt?" (Numbers 14:1–3 KJV)*

The Israelites acted in a way that many of us today do. They traveled all the way from the land of Egypt as they were in great suffering, pain, sorrow, and bondage. God supernaturally took care of them, but at the verge of entering the Promised Land, they allowed an evil report to get them discouraged. An evil report that caused them to weep, that cause them to stumble, that cause them to rebel against the God who has brought them out of their suffering place. They doubted the Word of God which has taken care of them. They allowed their faith to be tampered with. They followed the words *"I can't,"* or should I say *"they can't."* I want you to know that once you think and behave wrongly, your thoughts also go wrong and crazy. Through the negative report, their lives portray a lack of faith in God's Word for them. In life, I want us to know that just because we walk by faith, it is not a sign that we are not going to face any trials or tribulation and temptation. But that, through the Word of God (Bible), we are going to be more than conquerors over them.

> *"Nay, all told these things we are more than conquerors through him that loved us." (Romans 8:37 KJV)*

God has made numerous provisions available for His children to be able to possess their promised land. And even when we walk through what seems to be a wilderness, God provides a table of abundant provision for us. As long as you stay at the table of God's provision, even though the enemy is all around you, he cannot envelope you because he cannot come to that table. Speak faith-filled words. I will urge us to get a hold of the kind of faith in action. Joshua and Caleb were able to possess their Promised Land by what they said. They were determined to follow God and take Him at His word. They live their lives based on the faith that they have. Without faith in God, you do not have any shield of faith to hold up. Without faith, you will hinder the supernatural power of God from operating in your life like God has designed it to. Without faith in God, you are stripped of your defenses and you will be vulnerable to every attack that the enemy brings along. It takes faith to please God. It's not pleasing to God when you do not take Him at His Word. Those who had the faith of possessing their promised land among the children of Israelites were able to possess it. But those who doubted the Word of God, did not even see the promised land much less of possess it.

The Conquering Power of Faith

Faith is powerful. It is therefore powerful that an apostle of Christ may say: ***"This is the victory that has conquered the world, our faith" (1 John 5:4 CSB).*** Yet today throughout Christendom, the professed stronghold of this religion mentioned by the apostle, there is little evidence of any conquering power. For one factor, Christendom's faith is not conquering atheism. Without religion, it is impossible to win his (Jehovah's) good pleasure, for he that approaches God must believe that he is and that he becomes the rewarder of those earnestly seeking him. Faith is also needed because we must keep our eyes not on the things seen, but on the things unseen, and because faith is the power enabling one to triumph over the demon-controlled world. For your faith to work, you must learn to speak boldly like Jesus. Every single word that Jesus spoke when He was on this earth came to pass according to the said time he mentioned. Every time Jesus Christ opens His mouth to speak, He spoke the word of faith that produces an excellent result. Jesus Christ was crucified because of His words. Whenever He speaks, the blind were healed, the deaf hears, the lame walks, the maimed limb were made whole, and the dead rose up. His word was not ordinary, His words were different. His word carries power, authority, deliverance, and breakthrough. Whenever He speaks, significant changes take places in the lives of His hearer. God's words are very powerful, it can move the mountain. Jesus Christ knew who He was. He was never afraid of anything. Everyone marveled at Him whenever He speaks. He did not mince in declaring His word. Just like Jesus, the words we speak are spirit and they are life. Our religion is that the triumph that overcomes the globe. Our faith has supernatural power to tame, conquer and subdue the world. By faith, the folks crossed the Red Sea as if on land, but the Egyptians, when they attempted to do the same, were drowned. By faith, the walls of Jericho fell down when that they had been encircled for seven days. By religion, Rahab, the prostitute, failed to expose those that were disobedient, as a result, she had given a friendly welcome to the spies. The children of Israel marched around the city as instructed. There are many people today, both inside and outside the walls of the church, who have heard the message and fear the consequences of what they have heard but do not change their behavior accordingly. These are the people whom God calls "disobedient," and their lives will end in destruction. Rahab had faith in what she heard about God, and it produced in her the workings of the fruit of God's Holy Spirit. How easily we forget that the only thing that counts is faith working through love. It is one thing to believe what you have heard, and quite another to express that faith through love. As faith grows and develops, it must control the evil passions that threaten our spiritual peace by moving the mountain of Christ's kingdom into the present realities of life. Faith must also never shorten God's hands to perform all that He says, but continue to rely on the great Creator to fulfill all His declared work. And faith must give the personal courage to take the stumbling stones of personal offenses, and make them into the stepping stones of challenge and greater growth. By faith, we completely overcome the physical world. Noah was a man of faith; he found grace in the sight of God when God wanted to destroy the whole earth. Abraham also lived a life of faith. Everything in God's kingdom functions by the principle of faith. Everything about our life is hinged on our understanding of the word *"faith."* We need faith in our lives because our walk is a faith walk. Faith rests on divine testimony because beliefs are convictions that are held on the ground of divine testimony. Faith is a supernatural divine gift.

The subject of faith is not just a subject of prosperity or breakthrough that you are living both in time of your favor that you enjoy. Faith is necessary for both living and living victoriously. You cannot live a victorious life in this kingdom outside the operation of faith. Without faith, it is impossible to please God. The entire life of believers revolves around the word "faith." Some destinies have been affected in a lot of ways. By faith, Abel offered to God a more excellent sacrifice which God attested. God described faith as giving. It takes faith to be a giver. Enoch, the seventh man from creation, was translated by faith. By faith, Enoch left one level to another level, he translated from one territory to another territory. Every time that there is the manifestation of faith, God smiles. He is always happy. By faith men, maneuver situations. We have been so pampered that the system of faith is eroding in our minds. Faith is not hearing what God has said, but it is fulfilling your own part. There are some certain kinds of affliction that we need to go through as a result of faith. To make an impact in our generation, it must have to be by faith through faith. To get out of that sickness, problems, circumstances, situations, you need faith. You need to walk by faith with God. The Word of God is the instrument that produces faith. The word of God, whether spoken or written, contains the life of God. It is also a representation of commitment to the man. The Word of God also represents His will for man. The work of God is any communication or any platform where the voice of God, the ways of God, and the life of God can be accessed. It is our instrument for faith. Faith comes by preserving and hearing the Word of God. Faith also comes when you understand what you read.

Ways of Moving Your Mountains

As I have discussed earlier, you need to have faith and trust God's words for you to possess your promised land. Just as we have taken a look at the life of Caleb and Joshua and in how they applied the faith that made them reach their Promised Land. We are also going to take a look at life in the ways through which we can move our mountains. The ways through which your mountains can be moved will be examined below.

Wholly follow the Lord

Following God completely is important. Caleb wholly followed God. He totally dedicated himself to the things of God. He did everything that God told him to do. He believed what God said and also did what God said. He was in agreement with God in every area of life. He was completely committed to that thing and work of God. He didn't question or query God in everything that he was doing. He did not waiver from his God-given cause and purpose. This was the secret to Caleb's success. He possessed his mountain and was under a better covenant established upon better promises. He possessed his inheritance in Christ. Are you doing the same today? Do you follow God wholly or do you still doubt His Word? Do you work in agreement with God in every area of life like Caleb did? Have you totally dedicated yourself to God and to His work? To move your mountain in life, you need to totally dedicate and commit yourself to God, follow Him and His Word, obey His commandment, be in agreement with Him in that which you do, don't query or question His authority over your life. With this, you will be able to move those mountains that you are facing.

Speak the God kind of faith

The spirit of faith is the God kind of faith that believes and speaks out its faith in God in the midst of every impossible situation. Caleb knew how to believe God in his heart and speak faith with his mouth.

He believed the impossible could become possible when you have God. He never wavered from his confession. Caleb made himself dignified by his faith in God. God could depend on him to keep his thoughts and words in agreement with God. Can God depend on you today to get your thoughts and words in agreement with His Word? Have faith in God! Do not let your faith in God waver, have a persistent faith in God and His Word. Have the God kind of faith. When you have the God kind of faith, you will keep on believing God in the face of all your opposition or situations. Neither doubt nor disbelief God because doubt and unbelief will shut down every single faith that you have. Believing and confessing God's Word is God's inevitable law of faith. You need faith to move those mountains that you are facing. With faith in the Word of God and yourself, you will see yourself moving them easily.

Do not compromise

In moving your mountain, you need not comprise. Caleb was able to achieve his success in life because he never comprised. He was able to receive his inheritance because he never comprised his integrity before God or before men. Caleb set forth to accomplish what God has said even though he was detained and discouraged for many years. As we believe today, let's use the life of Caleb as an example when we are involving ourselves in an activity or when God gives us an assignment to carry out. You must not compromise His Word. Humble yourself and live right before God and quit doing some of the things that the world does. You need to realize now that the days of comprising are over. Stand uprightly and walk uprightly before God. Your victory will come when you follow God wholly, and you will be able to move your mountains.

Submit to godly leadership

Caleb's submission to Joshua's leadership was another reason for his success in God and his ability to possess what God has promised him. He totally submitted himself to Joshua as his leader and also followed all those instruction given to him by Joshua. He was able to bring the children of Israel into their Promised Land because he submitted himself to Joshua. As part of following God and moving your mountain so as to fulfill your dreams, you need to follow and submit to those leaders that God has chosen. Yes, you have a better qualification than they do, you are better looking than they are, and you work in a better place than they do, but you need to submit to their leadership. God has chosen them and you must wholly follow God and them for you to move your mountain and possess your promised land. Do not go about stirring up troubles, but rather stay calm and focused so that you will be able to move your mountain.

Penetrate those impossible barriers

When God delivered the children Israel from the hand of the Egyptians and told to them to go and possess their Promised Land; the only problem, or should I say, the only mountain between them and the Promise Land was the Jordan River. The Jordan River lay as an impossible barrier between them and the Promised Land. The children of Israel eventually crossed the Jordan River as a result of the victory God gave to them. Have you ever felt overwhelmed by the circumstances of life? Sometimes it seems as if these circumstances come in like a flood and try to sweep everything around us into its current, or it may sometimes feel as if you are hanging on for dear life. I would advise you to step on such circumstances. Hold on to the Word of God concerning your life, follow the instruction that God is giving to you and you will see that you will come out being triumphant. Through the Holy Spirit inside of you, you will be directed on how to get across every one of this flood or river. God has a solution for dealing with those flood waters of your life.

March victoriously on every "Jericho"

Jericho was a stronghold of the enemy and a fortress no one had been able to defeat. Many battles and many sieges had been fought at Jericho as enemies tried to conquer it but none had ever succeeded.

Jericho was the first battle that the Israelites encountered after they crossed the Jordan River to possess their Promised Land. The Israelites were able to conquer the wall of Jericho through the help of God. In life, we are going to encounter some spiritual Jericho just as the children of Israel did. In defeating this Jericho, you have to march victoriously on them by you trusting in the Word of God that He will give unto you victory over the Jericho of life. With the Word of God in your heart and in your mouth, you will be able to knock down every Jericho that seems to stand in your way to success.

Praise your way to victory

The Israelites, in order for them to defeat the wall of Jericho on the seventh day, blew the trumpet and shouted praises. They shouted the victory over the wall of Jericho. In that situation you are facing, you need to praise God, and in praising Him, let Him know. When you are confronted by any spiritual Jericho, begin to shout your way to victory, begin to praise God. Paul and Silas in the Bible were also confronted with spiritual Jericho. They were thrown into prison, but both of them prayed and praised God and they were both set free; they received their miracle. Whenever any adversary comes your way, just begin to stand on your ground and thank God. When you praise God, you come out of every situation victoriously. In that valley of the shadow of death, learn to praise Him. Learn to praise God even when fear confronts you on every side. Praise God when you are up against spiritual impossibilities, financial impossibilities, or any kind of impossibilities

Don't take sides against God

The enemy (devil) will try to steal everything he can from you. He will use every weapon he can to get you out of faith. He used doubt, fear, and unbelief to steal from the children of Israel. The Israelites could have gotten their confession in line with God's Word to them. They could have believed in their hearts and confessed faith in Him with their mouths. But they chose to doubt Him. Do not be like the

Israelites who sided against God. Do not take sides against the Word of God. Do not follow negative advises, because negative people will talk about what they do not believe. Do not allow your personalities to become negative through wrong thinking. Speak according to the will of God concerning your life because when you speak contrary to God's will, you hinder God from moving on your behalf. You must think in line with the Word of God.

Speak the Word over your situation

Believe what God's say in His Word. God will reward those who diligently seek Him and stand in faith on the integrity of His Word. To move your mountain, you have to stand on the Word of God, and apply the Word daily to every situation you are facing or passing through. Confess the Word! Yield to those instructions given to you by the Word and you will see yourself moving every unmovable mountain in your life and in your ministry.

The Factors Responsible for Delays in Mountain Moving

Moving your mountain requires you to be a faithful and diligent servant. You cannot just move your mountain if you are not in the right standing with God. God will not get involved in your situation if you do not harken unto His voice or His will. In moving your mountain, there are some factors that you need to get rid of because if you do not, they may serve as a hindrance for you in moving your mountain. Let take a look at these factors.

Disobedience

Disobedience can cost you your dream. The god that we serve is an awesome and mighty god. He has at His disposal such a bountiful reservoir of benefits, and He is just waiting to pour out His blessings upon us, as His children. Obedience to God's instructions and rules will help us receive what God has promised us in this life. Waiting before God in prayer and in His Word is what we must do. But sometimes it seems difficult for us just to take Him at His Word and obey Him. Obedience is a key to possessing our promised land in this life. What God has done for others, He will do for you if you just faithfully obey and have faith in Him. Moses could not enter either possess the Promised Land because of his disobedience to God. One of the reasons that we are not possessing that which belongs to us in Christ is that we are trying to do things in our own way, we are neglecting the help of the Almighty God, and as a result of that, we do not come out with outstanding success. You need to allow God to do what He wants to do in your life and when He wants to do it. Moses failed because of this. God told him exactly what He wanted him to do, but Moses did not do it according to God's way. Moses struck the rock in anger because the children of Israelites were complaining to Him. Moses harkened unto the voice of the children of Israel and this made him not to possess or enter the Promised Land. Disobedience will not make you achieve anything in life. God cannot honor a disobedient heart.

Wrong attitudes and motives

Today, many of us are standing on our mountain top for position of joining and seating with Christ. For you to be able to possess that which God has promised you, you need to stand and get in line with God in every area of your life. When you are with a wrong attitude, you cut off your blessings and prosperity in life. The wrong attitude hinders believers more than they realize from being able to receive from God. Sometimes, the wrong attitudes are thoughts of jealousy and envy. Our attitudes determine how far we can go with God. Attitude adjustments allow us to receive the blessing of God. God lifts up and promotes those whose attitudes and motives are pure. Let us rejoice with others when God blesses them because the same faithful God will also bless us too. Until you get your heart right with God, God will not be able to promote you in the ways He wants. A self-seeking attitude will eventually destroy a person's dreams. Don't try to take all the glory to yourself, causing others to look unto you instead of God. You cannot accomplish a thing without God. In every one of your achievement in life, give glory to God.

Doubts

Many believers continuously make their faith's confession, stating what they want to possess from God. But are they really possessing that which they want? In our lives, in one way or another, there is evidence of disobedience. There has been one way or another that, in our deed or in heart, we have disobeyed God's instruction. Disobedience, complaining, murmuring, and grumbling are all sin no matter how little they are. All these sins will keep us from receiving our promised land. If you find yourself in one situation or another, it is better to let people know your need than either complain or grumble. God has a time and purpose for each and every one of us, so, therefore, you do not get angry with God if your prayers are not answered promptly. Disobedience will cost you your promised land, but to successfully obtain promised land, we must walk in God's forgiveness and be washed in the blood of the Lord Jesus Christ.

You Are Made for a Reason

You are not an accident. Your birth was no mistake or mishap, and your life is not any fluke of nature. Your oldsters might not have planned to have you, however, God did. He wasn't in the least stunned by your birth. In fact, He expected it. God prescribed every single detail of your body. He deliberately selected your race, the color of your skin, your hair, and each alternative feature. He custom-made your body simply the approach He wished it. He conjointly determined the natural abilities you do possess and therefore the individuation of your temperament. God created you for a reason; he conjointly set your changed state and how long you live. He planned the times of your life before, choosing the exact time of your birth and death. God never will do something accidentally and He never makes mistakes. He has a reason for everything He creates, every plant and every animal. I was planned by God, and each person was designed with a purpose in mind. God's motive for creating you was His love. The Bible tells us, *"God is love."* It doesn't say "God has love." He is love!

Love is the essence of God's character. There is good love within the fellowship of the Trinity, so God didn't need to create you.

What Drives You

Fear

Many people are driven by fear. Their fears are also results of traumatic expertise, chimerical expectations, growing up in a very high-control home, or even genetic predisposition. Regardless of the cause, fear-driven people often miss great opportunities because they're afraid to venture out. Instead, they play it safe, avoiding risks and trying to maintain the status quo. Fear could be a voluntary jail that may keep you from changing into what God intends for you to be. You must move against it with the weapons of understanding, love, and the Word of God.

Anger

Many people are driven by resentment and anger. They hold on to hurts and never live through them. They practice their emotional pain over and over instead of forgiveness. Some resentment-driven folks "clam up" and assign their anger, while others "blow up" and explode it onto others. Both responses are unhealthy and unhelpful. Resentment continually hurts you over and over until you forgive that person you resent. While your wrongdoer has in all probability forgotten the offense and gone on with life, you continue to stew in your pain, perpetuating the past.

Guilt

Many people are driven by guilt. They live their entire lives running from regrets and concealing their shame. Guilt-driven people are manipulated by memories. They allow their past to control their future. They usually unconsciously penalize themselves by sabotaging their own success.

Material things

Many people are driven by the requirement for approval. They allow the expectations of oldsters, spouses, youngsters, lecturers, and friends to regulate their lives. Many adults are still making an attempt to earn the approval of unpleasable oldsters. Others are driven by peer pressure, always worried about what others might think. Unfortunately, those who follow the group typically stay in it.

Conclusion

In summary, in every one of our endeavors today, the north wind is totally there for us. It's there for our cleansing, deliverance, and redemption. Why not go back to your Father in heaven and ask Him to blow upon you the north wind piece of life.

Chapter 4

The South Wind—The Gentle Wind

The south wind brings quietness into the life of God's people when it blows. The wind makes man's spirit be quiet (gentle) before God, thereby allowing God to minister spiritual truth and revelation into the lives of His people. It is a wind of intimacy with God in terms of His Word, the Holy Spirit, the cross, with Jesus (the new man), with the mysteries of the kingdom, with the custodians of these mysteries.

"The Word became flesh and made his dwelling among us. We have seen his glory, the glory of the one and only Son, who came from the Father, full of grace and truth." (John 1:14 NIV)

The south wind is a wind that brings a time of refreshment or a new beginning into our lives as a result of the grace that we enjoyed that we are being called His children.

"Forget the former things; do not dwell on the past. See, I am doing a new thing! Now it springs up; do you not perceive it? I am making a way in the wilderness and streams in the wasteland." (Isaiah 43:18–19 NIV)

The south wind is a warm wind that brings good weather. "When ye see the south wind blow, ye say, There will be a heat; and it cometh to pass" *(Luke 12:55 KJV)*. It is a mild, balmy wind so the "earth is still by reason of the south wind" *(Job 37:17 ASV)*.

It is also a wind which ushers into our lives new season of abundant breakthrough, upliftment, and also gives us a new name.

"For Zion's sake I will be able to not keep silent, for Jerusalem's sake I will not remain quiet, till her vindication shines out like the dawn, her salvation like

a blazing torch. The nations will see your vindication, and all kings your glory; you will be called by a new name that the mouth of the Lord will bestow. You will be a crown of splendor in the Lord's hand, a royal diadem in the hand of your God" (Isaiah 63:1–3 NIV)

Job's life also experiences the refreshing south wind after the difficulties and challenges that he faced. The refreshing south wind will also blow on God's people who have endured to the end one persecution or another and are ready to become part of the kingdom of God.

"Repent, then, and turn to God, so that your sins may be wiped out, that times of refreshing may come from the Lord." (Act 3:19 NIV)

The south wind will also bring the peace of God which passes all understanding into the lives of God's people.

"And the peace of God which passeth all understanding, shall keep your heart and minds through Christ Jesus." (Philippians 4:7 KJV)

The south wind at times can be hot *(Luke 12:55)* or gentle *(Acts 27:13)*. In the gentle state of the south wind, it brings peace, quietness, and tranquility. "How thy are warm, when he quieteth the earth by the south wind?" *(Job 37:17 KJV)*

"He caused an east wind to blow in the heaven: and by his power, he brought in the south wind." (Psalm 78:26 KJV)

"...the south wind blew softly, supposing that they had obtained their purpose, loosing thence, they sailed close by Crete." (Acts 27:13 KJV)

When Job's three friends finished their discourse to him, the spirit-filled young man, Elihu, began to point out the things in Job's life that were displeasing before God. Elihu informed Job:

"How thy clothes are warm, when he quieteth the earth by the south wind?" (Job 37:17 KJV)

When the current of air blows, it will bring quietness to God's people. When man's spirit is quiet before God, God will minister spiritual truths unto His people. The current of air brings a time of refreshing in our lives. After Job's three religious friends were finished with their criticism of Job, Elihu, by the Spirit, brought the refreshing south wind into Job's life. After the east wind of God's judgment has blown upon the earth, the refreshing south wind will blow upon those who have endured unto the end and are predestined to become part of the kingdom of God. The apostle Peter, who was given the keys to the kingdom, spoke of those who will have prepared their lives for the times that are ahead of us:

"Repent ye therefore, and be converted, that your sins may be blotted out, when the times of refreshing shall come from the presence of the Lord..." (Acts 3:19 KJV)

Peter spoke of the times of refreshing. The times of refreshing from the presence of the Lord will come when the south wind blows upon the earth. The psalmist Asaph wrote:

"He caused an east wind to blow in the heaven: and by his power, he brought in the south wind." (Psalm 78:26 KJV)

After the east wind has blown upon the earth, God is going to bring forth the south wind. It will be a time of refreshing and release for God's people. The south wind will bring the peace of God that passeth all understanding (Philippians 4:7).

When Paul was to stand before Caesar, the king of the known world, the south wind became an important part of Paul's journey. Paul was falsely accused by the religious system of his day and was sent to Porcius Festus, the governor of Judah. Being a Roman citizen, Paul demanded to be tried before Caesar. Paul was then sent by ship from Caesarea to Rome to stand before Caesar. On this journey:

> *"...the south wind blew softly, supposing that they had obtained their purpose, loosing thence, they sailed by Crete." (Acts 27:13 KJV)*

Paul had a great time when the south wind blew in his life. Everything seemed to be going well on his trip. Paul had been assured by God he would stand before Caesar. Many today, like Paul, are not expecting any adversity. Their bellies are full, their bills are paid, the tank is full of gas, and there is money in the bank. How much better could it be? The south wind is blowing gently in their lives, and they are enjoying their complacency.

> *"But not long after there arose against it a tempestuous wind, called Euroclydon." (Acts 27:14 KJV)*

Paul encountered a severe storm called Euroclydon. The word "Euroclydon" comes from the Greek word *"euros"* and means "east wind." It means "a violent agitation." Those who have settled back on their lives, being refreshed by the south wind have not prepared their lives for the days ahead when the east wind will be released from the throne of God in all its fury. The east wind will bring judgment on all unrighteousness that exists not only on the earth but also in the earth. All God's people, like Paul, will stand before the King of the whole earth. The east wind will blow upon everyone, but God has promised the refreshing south wind that will blow upon His people. Paul was refreshed the second time by the south wind on his trip to Rome:

> *"And from thence we fetched a compass, and came to Rhegium: and after one day the south wind blew, and we came the next day to Puteoli..." (Acts 28:13 KJV)*

The south wind was to blow again upon Paul's journey. The south wind blew after one day. When we are finished with the Day of the Lord, the Day of Judgment in the earth, God's gentle south wind will again blow upon His people. When religious understanding is given, we have a tendency to understand how lovely God's guarantees are to Christians. We are in His hand, and nothing can hurt us, and no one can pluck us out of his nail-scarred hands.

Benefits of the South Wind

1. It's a wind that calms our souls to enjoy the moves of the Holy Spirit as He directs us in our daily living.
2. It ushers us into a new era of upliftment and breakthrough in life and in destiny.
3. It gives unto us eternal rest and reign with Christ Jesus.

Fulfilling Your Divine Destiny: The Gentle Wind

Divine destiny is the destiny of God in or for a man's life. It portrays the course of events in one's life, organized or structured by God to fulfill His divine purpose. Fulfilling your divine destiny is you living according to the will of God for your life. It also means doing what God is planning for your life. In fulfilling your divine destiny, your life becomes the expression of God's grace and the unveiling of His love. Everyone on this earth, both young and old, tall and short, who are Christians have a divine destiny to fulfill. God incorporates and arranges a purpose for our lives. We are not just created to only be on this earth alone, but we are created with a purpose, a will.

> *"'For I know the plans I have for you,' declares the Lord, 'plans to prosper you and not to harm you, plans to give you hope and a future'" (Jeremiah 29:11 NIV)*

God's plan for us is great, it's just it can be thwarted away by the evil ones or deprived us, thereby turning our lives upside down. In fulfilling your divine destiny, you first need to realize it yourself that you have a divine destiny. You can never fulfill what you don't think you have. In fulfilling your divine destiny, you need to change those pains and those sorrows that the devil has destined for us through our faith in God. You hold the key to your destiny and future. Through the blood of Jesus Christ shed for us on the cross of Calvary for redemption, we can have the faith to change our destiny while we are still on this earth. Blind Bartimaeus was faced with either the choice of fulfilling his destiny or not. But he chose to fulfill his God-given divine destiny for His life.

> *"And they came to Jericho: and as he went out of Jericho with his disciples and a great number of people, blind Bartimaeus, the son of Timaeus, sat by the highway side begging. And when he heard that it was Jesus of Nazareth, he began to cry out, and say, Jesus, thou son of David, have mercy on me. And many charged him that he should hold his peace: but he cried the more a great deal, Thou son of David, have mercy on me. And Jesus stood still, and commanded him to be called. And they called the blind man, saying unto him, Be of good comfort, rise; he calleth thee. And he, casting away his garment, rose, and came to Jesus. And Jesus answered and said unto him, What wilt thou that I should do unto thee? The blind man said unto him, Lord, that I might receive my sight. And Jesus said unto him, Go thy way; thy faith hath made thee whole. And immediately he received his sight, and followed Jesus in the way."*
> *(Mark 10:46–52 KJV)*

Bartimaeus's destiny was chosen for him through his circumstances—being blind. He was brought down to the lowest level through the situation he found himself in. On the day of God's visit to Jericho, Bartimaeus realized that this is his opportunity. Faith leapt in him when he heard the word that Jesus was passing by. Bartimaeus had in him the faith he needed to change his destiny in life. He made a choice of faith and his destiny was totally changed.

In fulfilling your divine destiny, don't let your natural man and sense make your decision and choice of direction for you.

> *"For to be carnally minded is death, but to be spiritually minded is life and peace." (Roman 8:6 KJV)*

You need to press on with God to fulfill your dreams and also feed on His Word, which will make your spirit stronger day by day. In doing things, find out the plan of God for that which you are to do before you embark on it.

In fulfilling your divine destiny, you also need to let go of the past; leave the past behind you and focus on what is ahead. When you look back to your past, you will never be able to fulfill your divine destiny.

> *"Brethren, I count not myself to have apprehended: but this one thing I do, forgetting those things which are behind, and reaching forth unto those things which are before, I press toward the mark for the prize of the high calling of God in Christ Jesus." (Philippians 3:13–14 KJV)*

In focusing on the future and forgetting the past, you need to be totally committed because it takes commitment to reach your divine destiny in life. Make commitment your first priorities; forget both the failures and successes of the past, walk on in the higher things of God and His Word.

In fulfilling your divine destiny, you also need to get acquainted with God. You need to know who God is before you study what plans He has for you. You need to listen to Him, take note of what He's saying to you through His Word. Reading His Word, praying to Him, talking with Him, and listening to Him are ways to get acquainted with God. Getting acquainted with Him needs the process of our spirit, not our mind. When your spirit comes in contact with God's spirit, you get acquainted with Him. When you get acquainted with God, you will be concerned about the things of the Father and about others instead of just yourself. You will realize that all that you have been taken care of. In getting acquainted with God, you realize and also receive from God the good gifts of salvation, healing, and prosperity. When you get acquainted with God, you will have all your desires and needs met by Him.

> *"And my God shall supply all your need according to his riches in glory by Christ Jesus." (Philippians 4:19 KJV)*

In fulfilling your divine destiny, you need to attend to God's Word. The amount of attention you give to the Bible will determine whether or not you fulfill your divine destiny. So, therefore, meditate on the Word. Meditating on the Word is not just for some few minutes but having a deeper understanding of what the Word says. When you meditate on God's Word, you get wisdom to do all things. Wisdom is necessary in all areas of life, even in the business world. If wisdom abounds, you will operate your business perfectly and wisely. If you don't have any wisdom, you will operate your business imperfectly and unwisely, and it will lead to the failure of such business. Get the wisdom and the understanding of the Word to fulfill your destiny.

To fulfill your divine destiny, you also need to practice the Word. Don't not only meditate on the Word but practice it. Put what you have learned from the Word into use. Daily apply what the Word says or what the Word talks about into your life and you will see that things are working your way. Don't just read or meditate on the Word, you assume through it and you will be divinely blessed. You need to take the step of faith by putting into the use what you have learned or heard from the Word to be successful in life.

In fulfilling your divine destiny, God also needs you to put the Word first in your life and become Word-conscious. Let the Word reign supreme in your life. No matter what comes your way, think first about the Word, what it says concerning that situation. In times of trials and tribulations, the Word you have in you will start recalling to your pertinent scriptures about such trials or tribulations.

In fulfilling your divine destiny, you also need to be led by the spirit of God. You need to instantly obey the voice of God. God leads us by our spirit, not by our mind. Through this, God informs our spirit, which, in turn, informs our minds. For you to be successful in life, you need to learn how to be led by the voice of God. Do that which the Lord is telling you to do. Get informed immediately in that which the Lord is telling you to do, you can carry it out perfectly.

Learning to forgive is also another prominent way for us to fulfill our divine destiny in life. You need to forgive and forget that wrong which was done against you and make peace with the person that has wronged you. In forgiving and forgetting, you need to love such individual wholeheartedly and also correct him on the wrong which he has done against you. The person who wronged you has to answer to God. You cannot answer for him or her but all you need to do is just to forgive them and pray for them. Without forgiveness, it is impossible to make your faith works. And you need your faith to work for you to fulfill your divine destiny in life.

In fulfilling your divine destiny, you also need to purge your conscience with the blood of Christ. Receiving answers from God is not difficult as many have supposed it to be. However, a clouded mind finds it difficult to discern the source of information coming to it, thereby failing to know whether God has answered or not. You will need to purge your conscience from dead works of selfishness and fear. Blot out every selfishly generated desire and demonic fear from your mind.

Paying attention to your desire is also one of the ways through which you can fulfill your divine destiny in life. When you have the proper frame of mind and your motives are to glorify the name of Israel, you will develop heartfelt desires to do something. Those strong desires define your divine destiny.

> *"For it is God which worketh in you both to will and to do of his good pleasure." (Philippians 2:13 KJV)*

In fulfilling your destiny, you need to also have the right motives. Don't ask amiss, ask according to the perfect will of God for your life. You must ask with the simplicity of heart. Let the name of God be glorified in that which you are asking. You will discover that financial prosperity, salvation, healing, promotion, and the good things that we are craving to come easily when the name of Christ will be exalted through them.

In fulfilling your destiny, you also need to decide for yourself what is worthy of your pursuit. No one else should decide for you, neither can anyone decide for you. You may receive counsel from others, however, you ought to build the decision, otherwise, you'll be unrealized in your pursuit. There are innumerable stories of men who achieved great success, nonetheless, their destiny remained unrealized because they were living another person's dream. Don't live another man's dream. Live and decide your own dream so that you can fulfill your destiny. Being time conscious is another fact that you need to know so that you can achieve or fulfill your destiny. God gave you time for all you have to do and you are responsible for making use of your time and your life to do all you have to do for God. You can't do everything! You can't go everywhere! Your life is packaged in capsules of time. Whom you spend your time with and how you spend your time is actually taking your life. Anyone who wastes your time is wasting your life. Be wise in how you spend your time.

In fulfilling your divine destiny, you need to be focused on God. One purpose of circumstances is that God might prove His power and glory to a world that needs to see His majesty. Another purpose is that He might prove Himself to you in such a way that you will learn to trust Him with utter confidence despite the gravity of the circumstances around you. God is sufficient for your circumstances. He will be faithful in every circumstance of your today and your tomorrows. You can be assured of this because He already has proven Himself faithful in the problems of yesterday. God uses every situation to demonstrate His power and glory and to prepare you to fulfill your destiny. Your circumstances actually work for you when you keep your focus on their eternal benefits.

"For our light affliction, which is but for a moment, worketh for us a far more exceeding and eternal weight of glory..." (2 Corinthians 4:17 KJV)

"For we know that if our earthly house of this tabernacle were dissolved, we have a building of God, an house not made with hands, eternal in the heavens." (2 Corinthians 5:1 KJV)

In fulfilling your divine destiny, you need also to change your thinking habit. Despite the problems you are facing today, do not look to the size of your need, but look to the size of your god. Satan brings negative circumstances into your life so that we can focus on it instead of focusing on God. When you worry about your problems, you eventually develop spiritually blinding cataracts that can keep you from seeing the Word at work in your life. Do not look at your need. Do not look at your problem. Focus on God and the promises in His Word. There are some many people who seem to focus only on their problems. They have looked so long at their problems that their difficulties have become like mountains in their eye, roofing out everything else. They cannot talk about anything else and they do not think about anything else. It actually seems like they do not want to part with their problems because they hold on to them so tightly. It is almost impossible to get such people to turn their eyes on Jesus because they seemingly do not trust God enough to relinquish their troubles to Him. It is time for you to change your focus. Your problems are hindrances to seeing God's abilities. Look to the One who is above all, greater than all, and mighty enough to empower you to meet every situation that you face. If you are facing a monumental task today, know that He will lead you each step of the way, and each step will be a miracle.

Another factor that is important for you in fulfilling your divine destiny is for you to climb every of your mountain such as the mountain of debts, mountain of fear, the mountain of sin, and bondage, the mountain of sickness and the mountain of the broken relationship. God's power is greater than your mountain. When you know that God's Word is the final word, you will not focus on your mountains or listen to the negative words of others regarding your situation. You will rise up and begin to exploit like you have never experienced in your life. You will believe in God, belief in His miracles concerning

83

that situation, and you will also believe in His voice concerning that mountain. His voice will give you direction in life. Through His Word, you would be able to move your mountains.

In order to fulfill God's will for your life, you must live out His will for each day. It is God's will to save every person from sin. God wants us to experience salvation, provision, health, and victory and it is important to know that it is His will for you to have these blessings. God wants us to be a good servant, doing His will from our heart. He wants us to be perfect and complete in *Him*. It is His will that we give Him thanks in everything that we do. It is His will that the works you do for Him silence the ignorance of foolish men. God wants you to no longer live by the lusts of the flesh, but by the will of God. God is looking for men and women who will remain true to their vision. Abraham caught a vision and never looked back. Moses was able to lead Israel to the edge of their Promised Land because he had a vision. Joshua and Caleb held on to their visions for forty long years in the wilderness as their generation perished. Paul's vision became the main focus of his life. It was the driving force that compelled him to endure hardship, persecution, discouragement, shipwreck, and physical abuse. It motivated his writing. It directed his travels. It dictated his lifestyle. Let your vision be clear and let it be the driving force behind every one of your success or failures.

> *"That he no longer should live the rest of [his] time in the flesh to the lusts of men, but to the will of God."*
> *(1 Peter 4:2 WBT)*

> *"For so is the will of God, that with well doing ye may put to silence the ignorance of foolish men."*
> *(1 Peter 2:15 KJV)*

> *"In everything give thanks: for this is the will of God in Christ Jesus to you-ward." (1 Thessalonians 5:18 ASV)*

In fulfilling your divine destiny in life, you also need to develop consistent faith in the word of God. You need to realize that there is nothing in yourself other than what you receive from the heavenly places. It is not your joy, but it is Christ's joy, which is being manifested in you. It is not your peace, but it is Christ's peace. It is not your love; it is the love of God extended through you to others. It is not your faith that produces the power needed to fulfill your destiny. If you cannot produce love, joy, or peace, why do you think that you can produce faith to achieve your destiny? Your faith is consistent because it is God's faith extended through the *vine* (Jesus) to the branch (you) to produce the spiritual fruit of love, joy, peace, faith, etc. You will be able to live a consistent life because it is God's faith extended to you, flowing in you, and through you from the true vine, Jesus Christ.

> *"I am the vine, ye are the branches: He that abideth in me, and that I in him, the same bringeth forth much fruit: for without me ye can do nothing." (John 15:5 KJV)*

In fulfilling your divine destiny, you need to have the power in the presence of God. The presence of God includes:

God's omnipresence: God is always presented everywhere.

God's indwelling presence: when you accepted Jesus as Savior, the Holy Spirit came to live within you.

God's manifested presence: when God reveals Himself in a given time and place in a way you can discern with your physical and spiritual senses.

God's *Shekinah* presence: God dwells continuously in a given location as He did in the Old Testament tabernacle.

When God's presence is with you, you will have no fear, neither will you be intimidated. You will not be afraid of wicked governments. You won't be concerned if they say preaching the gospel is against the law. You will not be concerned if they say you cannot distribute religious materials or convert people to the Lord Jesus Christ. The presence of God is your secret weapon against intimidation. The presence of God is your ultimate spiritual weapon. When the presence of God is manifested in your life, you will not be afraid of what people say about you. You will not worry about what the world says. People will not be able to affect you, cut you down, or destroy you emotionally by their opinions, comments, or actions. Many of us are burdened down by guilt and condemnation over the past. The presence of God in you breaks these yokes of guilt and condemnation. When God's presence is with you, you will pass through deep waters, but you will not be drowned. You may be forced to walk into the fiery furnace, but you will not be burned. You may be thrown into a lion's den, but the animals will not harm you. They may prowl around, roar, and try to intimidate but they cannot and will not be able to harm you. When God's presence is with you, like Elijah, you will be able to face the false prophets of Baal and emerge victoriously. You will be able to confront criticizing, backbiting, rebellious people. You will be able to courageously advance into enemy territory with authority because you know you cannot be defeated. With the presence of God with you, you can march right in and rescue people from the very gates of hell because you have the ultimate weapon: God's divine presence! With God's presence abiding in you, you can go through any flood, you can emerge unscathed from the fire, and you can endure any trial. You will not merely survive; you will come through victoriously because His presence is with you! The presence of God removes all fear, intimidation, and all condemnation. His presence prepares you to impact the world. This presence of God will take you to places you never thought you would go. God's presence equips you, protects you, and provides guidance. His presence strengthens you and separates you from the world. It heals, renews, and cleanses you. It empowers your destiny. It has unlimited power. That is why you must have His presence.

In fulfilling your divine destiny, you need to be more careful of your conducts, anointing, and characters towards the things of God. God wants you to be faithful: faithful to your spouse, your boss, pastors, faithful in that which we do, faithful in your work place, faithful to the things of His, and faithful to your destiny. God wants a faithful servant. He wants us to possess the Christ-like character in that which we do. He wants us to use those resources well that have been diligently and faithfully committed into our hands. He wants us to live a reputable life.

Fulfilling Your Dream: Building Strong Faith

Only strong faith will triumph over every situation and circumstances. It is strong faith that takes back what the devils have stolen from you. And it is strong faith that turns your destiny into a reality. In fulfilling your divine destiny, you need to build a strong faith in God and here are some of the steps you need in building a strong faith in God.

Surround yourself with that which produces faith

Every Christian has received the measure of faith from God. You need to use this measure of faith in your circumstance after salvation has come to you. Many Christians today surround themselves with things that cause them to be in the faith. They sit in a church that does not teach the Word of God, listening to all manner and kinds of thing that cannot build up their faith. For you to nurture your faith and build that which will produce a result for your destiny, you must surround yourself with successful people of God and also feed your mind and spirit on the things that will build your faith in God. Surround yourself with things of faith and don't live a negative life.

Build on God's Word, not on experience

In fulfilling your divine destiny, you need to build on the Word of God. Jesus did not build his work on experience, but He builds Himself and works on the Word that He was taught. Do not have the perspective that, since you have experience in that situation, you can overcome it through your knowledge or experience on it. Building on experience might or will sink you down and will also deprive you of achieving your divine destiny. So, therefore, for you to succeed in life, build yourself on the Word of God. Daily surround yourself with that which we have learned from the Word. Daily get yourself acquainted with the do's and don'ts of the Word that you have learned. Daily add the value of the Word that you have read and apply them to your existence.

Obedience is necessary

Fulfilling your divine destiny requires you to be an obedient child. In being obedient, you are required to walk in the light of the eternal Word of God. In walking in this light, you have the confidence and know that which has been said, he will do and thus you have the right to claim them. We need to constantly live in the right sight of God and constantly do what He asked us to do.

You must be humble

Be of good behavior, don't be proud, have a submissive heart. Don't portray yourself as someone who knows all. Be humble before God and before man, and behave as if you knew nothing so that you can achieve that which you want.

You must have holy boldness

You have to be bold in that which you do. Boldly take that which you need from God. Boldly pronounce your deliverance in those areas of healing, finance, sorrow, pain, or whatever it may be. Boldly begin to proclaim that which is yours according to God's will for your life. Don't be afraid of the devil. He has no power over you. Be authoritative in the way you deal with him (the devil). Boldly open your mouth and prophesize that which you want into your life.

Fulfilling Your Dream: Planned For God Pleasure

We are planned for God's pleasure. The moment you we were born into the world, God was there as an unseen witness, smiling at our birth. He wanted you alive, and your arrival gave Him great pleasure. God did not need to create us, but He chose to create us for His own enjoyment. We exist for His profit, His glory, His purpose, and His delight. Bringing enjoyment to God, living for His pleasure, is the first purpose of your life. When we fully understand this truth, you will never again have a problem with feeling insignificant. It proves your worth. If you're that necessary to God, and He considers you valuable enough to keep with Him for eternity. What greater significance could you have? You are God's baby, and you bring pleasure to God like nothing else He has ever created.

One of the best gifts God has given America is the ability to get pleasure from pleasure. He wired us with five senses and emotions so you can experience it. He wants us to enjoy life, not just endure it. The reason you're ready to get pleasure from pleasure is that God created you in His image. We often forget that God has emotions too. He feels things very deeply. We were told in the Bible that God grieves, gets jealous and angry, and feels compassion, pity, sorrow, and sympathy as well as happiness, gladness, and satisfaction. God loves, delights, gets pleasure, rejoices, enjoys, and even laughs. The smile of God is the goal of your life. Since pleasing God is our first purpose in life, your most important task is to discover how to do that. The Bible says, "Figure out what's going to please Christ, and then do it." Fortunately, the Bible gives us a clear example of a life that gives pleasure to God. The man's name was Noah. In Noah's day, the entire world had become morally corrupt. Everyone lived for their own pleasure, not God's pleasure. God couldn't find anyone on earth interested in pleasing Him, so He was grieved and regretted making a man. God became therefore fed up with the mankind that He thought about wiping it out. The Bible says, "Noah was a pleasure to the Lord." God said, "This guy brings a state pleasure. He makes me smile. I'll begin over together with his family." From his life, we learn the five acts of worship that make God smile. Noah treasured God quite against anything within the world, even when no one else did. The Bible tells us that for his entire life, *"Noah consistently followed God's will and enjoyed a close relationship with Him."* This is what God wants most from you: a relationship. It is the most astounding truth in the universe that our Creator wants to fellowship with us. God made you, love you, and he longs for you to love Him back. He says, *"I don't want your sacrifices—I to want your love; I don't want your offerings—I to want you to know me."* God deeply loves you and desires your love in return. He longs for you to understand Him and pay time with Him. This is why learning to like God and be treasured by Him ought to be the best objective of your life. God smiles at us when we do the following:

God smiles when we trust Him completely

Noah was able to please God because He trusted God, even when it did not make sense. By faith, Noah engineered a ship within the middle of the land. He was warned about something he could not see and acted on what he was told. As a result, Noah became intimate with God. God was displeased with the whole world, but Noah found favor and grace in the sight of God. God instructed him to build a giant ship that will save him and his entire family and the animals. There were three issues that would have caused Noah to doubt. First, Noah had never seen rain, because prior to the flood, God irrigated the earth from the ground up. Second, Noah lived many miles from the closest ocean. Even if he may learn to create a ship, how would he get it to water? Third, there was the matter of miscalculating up all the animals and also caring for them. But Noah did not complain nor murmur, neither did he make excuses. Trusting God utterly means that having a religion that he is aware of what's best for our life. We expect Him to keep His promises, help you with problems, and do the impossible when necessary.

God smiles when we obey Him wholeheartedly

Saving the animal population from a worldwide flood needed careful attention to supplying and detail. Everything had to be done even as God prescribed it. God gave Noah very detailed instructions as to the size, shape, and materials of the ark as well as the different numbers of animals to be brought on board. Noah did everything exactly as God commanded and instructed him. God does not owe you an explanation or reason for everything he asks you to do. Understanding can wait, but obedience cannot. Instant obedience can teach you additional lessons regarding God than a period of Bible discussions. In fact, you may never perceive some commands till you confirm them initially. Obedience unlocks understanding. Often, we try to offer God partial obedience. We want to and choose the commands we tend to conform.

God smiles after we praise and give thanks to Him frequently

Few things feel higher than receiving sincere praise and appreciation from somebody else. God loves it too. God smiles after we categorize our adoration and feeling to Him. Noah's life brought pleasure to God as a result of the life he lived, with a heart of praise and thanksgiving. Noah's initial act once living the flood was too precise his due to God by providing a sacrifice. An amazing a thing happens when we offer praise and thanksgiving to God. When we give God enjoyment, our own hearts are filled with joy. Worshipping God works both ways too. We enjoy what God has done for us and when we express that enjoyment to God, it brings Him joy, but it also increases our joy.

God smiles when we use our abilities

Sometimes we feel that the only time God is pleased with us is when we are doing "spiritual" activities like reading the Bible, attending church, praying, or sharing our faith. And we may think God is unconcerned about the other parts of your life. Actually, God enjoys watching every detail of your life, whether you are working, playing, resting, or eating. He does not miss a single move we make. Every human activity, except sin, can be done for God's pleasure if we do it with an attitude of praise. We can wash dishes, repair a machine, sell a product, write a computer program, grow a crop, and raise a family for God's glory. God especially enjoys watching us use our talents and abilities that He gave to us. God intentionally gifted us differently for His enjoyment. He has made some to be athletic and some to be analytical. You may be gifted at mechanics or mathematics or music or a thousand other skills. All these abilities bring a smile to God's face. You do not bring glory or pleasure to God by hiding your abilities or by trying to be someone else. You can only bring Him enjoyment by being you. Anytime you reject any part of yourself, you are rejecting God's wisdom and sovereignty in creating you.

Conclusion

In summary, God's gentle wind will again blow on us as His people. We are then going to enjoy all the promises of God because we are in His hand and nothing can either hurt us neither plucks us out of His presence.

Chapter 5

The West Wind—The Stormwind

T he west wind is the wind that will make known the end of the day or the end of the age and will bring about the restoration of all things. The west wind ushers the returns of new things. Through the blowing of the west wind, God will totally restore the earth back to those days of His creation. The west wind blows from the setting of the sun which represents the end of the age. The west wind brought back to the Egyptian a time of restoration after the locust totally destroyed everything.

> *"And the Lord changed the wind to a very strong wind, which caught up the locusts and carried them into the Red Sea. Not a locust was left anywhere in Egypt." (Exodus 10:19 NIV)*

God's plan of restoration on earth after the great locusts was no more. The time of this restoration will usher a new beginning. It will bring with it a moment of happiness.

The west winds bring the restoration of all things after God's judgment. All those things that have made us be devastated in one way or another would be removed and replaced by those that bring glory and honor to God's name.

> *"And this is for your benefit, so that the grace that is reaching more and more people may cause thanksgiving to overflow to the glory of God." (2 Corinthians 4:15 NIV)*

The west wind also demonstrates the saving grace of God. After the anointment of King David, the Israelite was faced by the army of the Philistine because they want to be in control over Israel. God gave David some specific instructions which he followed faithfully and he greatly defeated the Philistine.

> *"The Philistines also went and deployed themselves in the Valley of Rephaim. So David inquired of the Lord, saying, 'Shall I go up against the Philistines? Will you deliver them into my hand?' And the Lord said to David, 'Go up, for I will doubtedless deliver the Philistines into your hand.' So David went to Baal Perazim, and defeated them there; and he said, 'The Lord has broken through my enemies before me, like a breakthrough of water.' Therefore he called the name of the place Baal Perazim. And they left their images there, and David and his men carried them away. Then the Philistines went up once again deployed themselves in the Valley of Rephaim. Therefor David inquired of the Lord, and He said, 'You shall not go up; circle around behind them, and come upon them in front of the mulberry trees. And it shall be, when you hear the sound of marching in the tops of the mulberry trees, then you shall advance quickly. For then the Lord will go out before you to strike the camp of the Philistines.' And David did so, as the Lord commanded him; and he drove back the Philistines from Geba as far as Gezer." (2 Samuel 5:18–25 NKJV)*

When you follow the moves of the Spirit of God, the wind of God will make you be successful in that which you do or lay your hands upon. Through the west wind, the earth shall be renewed and the original plan of God for mankind will thus be fulfilled. It is a driving wind that drives away difficulties, the hardship that is facing us in one way or another.

> *"And the Lord turned a mighty strong west wind, which took away the locusts and cast them into the Red Sea; there remained not one locust in all the coasts of Egypt." (Exodus 10:19 KJV)*

The west wind is most commonly blown in Palestine. It comes from the sea and carries the moisture which condenses to form clouds, turned upward by the mountains, to the cooler layers of the atmosphere. Elijah looked toward the west for the "small cloud," and soon *"the heavens grew black with clouds and wind" (1 Kings 18:44). "When ye see a cloud rise out of the west, straightway ye say, There cometh a shower; and so it is" (Luke 12:54 KJV).*

The west wind is the wind that brings rain, a remedy for the east wind, it is refreshing. The west wind blows from the setting of the sun and reveals the end of the day, even restoration of all things. *Exodus 10:19 KJV, "And the LORD turned a mighty strong west wind, which took away the locusts and cast them into the Red sea...."*

There is one more wind that must blow upon the earth, and that is the west wind. The west wind displays the times of restoration. When the west wind blows, God will restore the earth as it was in the day of His creation. The west wind only appears once in the Bible. The west wind blows from the setting of the sun. This represents the end of the age. When God sent the plague of locusts, every green thing was destroyed in Egypt. Moses recorded:

> *"For they covered the face of the whole earth, so that the land was darkened; and they did ate every herb of the land and all the fruit of the trees that the hail had left. So there remained nothing green on the trees or on the plants of the field throughout all the land of Egypt." (Exodus 10:15 NKJV)*

The locusts brought total destruction upon Egypt. But God has promised to send deliverance and restoration upon Egypt. Moses revealed:

> *"And the Lord turned a mighty strong west wind, which took away the locusts, and cast them into the Red Sea; there remained not one locust in all the coasts of Egypt." (Exodus 10:19 KJV)*

When the locusts were removed, God's plan of restoration began to take place and the earth was restored. Jesus revealed another plague like the locusts that He would send upon the earth in the time of His judgment.

> *"And there came out of the smoke locusts upon the earth: and unto them was given power, because the scorpions of the earth have power. And it was commanded them that they should not hurt the grass of the earth, neither any green thing, neither any tree; but only those men which have not the seal of God in their foreheads. And to them it was given that they should not kill them, but that they should be tormented five months: and their torment was as the torment of a scorpion, when he striketh a man. And in those days shall men seek death, and shall not find it; and shall desire to die, and death shall flee from them." (Revelation 9:3–6 KJV)*

These stinging locusts would torment men five months. Men wanted to die, but death will not be available to them. Man's only relief will come from God. Those who apply God's promises to their lives will be spared and those who reject God's Word will perish. Israel was given to us as an example. We need to view Israel as to what God will accomplish in the earth at the end of the age. Those who know their God and walk in His ways can expect the west wind to blow in their lives. The west wind brings the restoration of all things after the judgment of God. All the things that have brought devastation to our lives will be removed. Only those things that bring glory to the Father will remain. The mighty wind of the Spirit, alone, will bring salvation to God's people.

God's Judgment

Today many are teaching the judgment of God is not for His people. We need to realize if there were no judgment, there would be no purified body of Christ. Those who teach this error have completely overlooked many scriptures in the New Testament. They have disregarded the types and shadows of God's judgment upon Israel. We must not disregard the words of Paul who revealed:

"Now all these things happened unto them for examples: and they are written for our admonition, upon whom the ends of the world are come." (1 Corinthians 10:11 KJV)

The apostle Peter also proclaimed the coming judgment very clearly:

"For the time is come that judgment must begin at the house of God: and if first begin at us, what shall the end be of them that obey not the gospel of God." (1 Peter 4:17 KJV)

Peter, by the Spirit, forewarned all who would read to understand that judgment must begin at the house of God. He then asked the question, "What shall the tip be for people who adapt not the gospel of God?" This is not written to the world because God does not expect the worldly people to obey His gospel. This is written to those who are called by His name. God is going to judge His whole house. The severity of God's wind of judgment will be determined by where we stand with the Lord. Has the gospel changed our lives? Have we obeyed the gospel? Many believe because they follow the dictates of their religious order, they are accepted by their God, they have become legalistic in their beliefs. Paul warned all who desire to keep the law, either Moses's law or man's law:

"Christ is become of no effect unto you, whosoever of you are justified by the law; ye are fallen from grace." (Galatians 5:4 KJV)

Those who are justified by the law have fallen from grace. We have God's promise that His judgment will fall upon those who do not obey the gospel. Grace is the unmerited, loving favor and graciousness

97

of our Creator. It is an important aspect of God's character and nature, abounding and overflowing outwardly in acts of mercy, compassion and liberal giving. The apostle Peter called God "the God of all grace" (1 Peter 5:10). As a free gift, God bestows His grace upon us. How does He do that? We receive God's gift of grace through faith in Jesus Christ's sacrifice—His shed blood.

The Wind on Top of the Mulberry Trees

God used the wind many times in His Word to demonstrate His saving grace. There was a time when the Philistine army came against Israel. This was soon after David was anointed king. The Philistines thought they could unseat the newly crowned king and be in control of all Israel. Although David was victorious, the Philistines would try again:

> *"Therefore David enquired again of God; and God said unto him, Go not up after them; turn away from them, and come upon them over against the mulberry trees.*
> *And it shall be, when thou shalt hear a sound of going in the tops of the mulberry trees, that then thou shalt go out to battle: for God is gone forth before thee to smite the host of the Philistines." (1 Chronicles 14:14–15 KJV)*

God gave David specific instructions. He was to circle around and come up behind the enemy. He was to encamp next to the mulberry trees. There were probably other kinds of trees there. But God did not speak to David to go to any tree. He gave David direct orders. If the wind of the Lord is going to blow in our lives we need to:

1. Know His voice
2. Listen for His voice
3. Be obedient to His voice

David was told, "When thou shalt hear a sound of going in the tops of the mulberry trees..." then he was to attack not before, nor after. We need to raise, "What was moving in the tops of the mulberry trees?" It was the wind of the Lord. The word wind is *ruwach* and means "breath or spirit." It was the Spirit that was moving in the tops of the mulberry trees. It did not blow in any of the other trees, only the mulberry. God is wanting us to recognize the move of His Spirit. When David went up, he was successful because he followed the move of the Spirit of God, the wind of the Lord.

Contrary Winds

There came a time when Jesus had to deal with the wind in His disciples' lives. After Jesus fed the five thousand:

> *"...straightway he constrained his disciples to get into the ship, and to go to the other side before unto Bethsaida, while he sent away the people."* *(Mark 6:45 KJV)*

> *"And he saw them toiling in rowing; for the wind was contrary unto them: and about the fourth watch of the night he cometh unto them, walking upon the sea, and would have passed them." (Mark 6:48 KJV)*

The disciples were toiling in rowing, trying to get to where they wanted to go. But the wind was contrary unto them. Many today who think they are walking in the Spirit find the wind of the Lord is contrary to them. They are trying to get to where they want to go or do what they want to do. Jesus is always nearby, walking upon the sea, but He will continue to pass them by until they call out to Him.

> *"For they all saw him, and were troubled. And immediately he talked with them, and saith unto them, Be of good cheer: it is I; be not afraid. And he went up unto them into the ship; and the wind ceased: and*

they were sore amazed in themselves beyond measure, and wondered." (Mark 6:50–51 KJV)

The disciples were troubled when they saw Jesus. They thought they were all alone in their tribulation. They did everything humanly possible to solve their dilemma. It only took a word from the Lord, and their troubled sea was calm. There was another instance when Jesus's disciples were on the troubled sea:

> *"And, behold, there arose a great tempest within the sea, insomuch that the ship was covered with the waves: but he was asleep. And his disciples came to him, and awoke him, saying, Lord, save us: we perish. And he saith unto them, Why are ye fearful, O ye of little faith? Then he arose, and rebuked the winds and the sea; and there was a great calm. But the lads marveled, saying, What manner of man is this, that even the winds and the sea obey him!" (Matthew 8:24–27 KJV)*

When we are going through the storms of life, we may think many times God is asleep, or just simply not concerned about what we are going through. When our ship is covered with water, and we think we are going to sink, this is when we desire to get God's attention. When everything is going well, and we have smooth sailing journey, sometimes God gets in our way and we would not care if He took a nap and left us alone. We are our own helmsmen and we do not need any help. But let the storm arise and our need for God arises very quickly, and we begin to seek His presence. The disciples got Jesus's attention, and He arose and rebuked the contrary wind in their lives, and there was a great calm. The peace that passeth all understanding returned to their lives. When we are going through a difficult storm in our life, all we need is a word from the Lord and our storms become a great calm. We marvel, saying, "What manner of man is that this, that the wind and the sea obey Him?" If the disciples had known the Word of God, they would not have been surprised because the psalmist wrote:

> *"He maketh the storm calm, so that the waves thereof are still." (Psalm 107:29 KJV)*

When the wind of the Lord is contrary in our lives, then we are not going with the wind, but contrary to the wind. We are desiring to go our own way. When the wind is contrary, the Lord is attempting to change our direction to walk with Him. When we change directions, then the wind will be at our backs and our sails will be full, and our journey easy. When we are going against the wind, our toiling becomes impossible. When we call Christ into our ship and make Him our helmsman, we will reach His destination in our life. The continuously whirling north wind and south wind will calm our seas and bring the deliverance the Lord has promised. Praise will return to our lips, and joy will return to our heart.

God's Spiritual Wind

Jesus addressed the wind when Nicodemus came to Him in the night:

> *". . .and same unto Him, "Rabbi, we know that Thou art a teacher come from God: for no man can do these miracles that thou doest, except God be with him." (John 3:2 KJV)*

Jesus's answer to Nicodemus was:

> *"Except a man be born again, he cannot see the kingdom of God." (John 3:3 KJV)*

The word "see" is the Greek word *eido*. It is derived from the Latin word "video" and means "to perceive with the eyes." Another meaning is "to know." Nicodemus's reply was:

> *"How can a man be born when he is old? Can he enter*
> *the second time into his mother's womb, and be born?*
> *   Jesus answered, Verily, verily, I say unto thee, Except*
> *a man be born of water and of the Spirit, he cannot enter*
> *into the kingdom of God." (John 3:4–5 KJV)*

Jesus's answer was, "Except an individual be born of water and of the Spirit, he cannot enter into the dominion of God." There is a big difference in seeing the kingdom of God and entering into the kingdom. Many who can see the kingdom will never enter because they have not been born of water, nor the Spirit. When we have been truly born of water, the old man has been dealt with. In his letter to the Romans, Paul explained the purpose of water baptism:

> *"Knowing this, that our old man is crucified with him,*
> *that the body of sin might be destroyed, that henceforth*
> *we should not serve sin." (Romans 6:6 KJV)*

When we are born of water, the old man is crucified, the body of sin is destroyed, and we are no longer a servant of sin or the old sin nature. This is a continuing process in our life. The act of baptism is only a commitment to allow God, through the Holy Spirit, to change our lives. The apostle Peter informed us:

> *"Repent, and be baptized every one of you in the name*
> *of Jesus Christ for the remission of sins, and ye shall*
> *receive the gift of the Holy Ghost." (Acts 2:38 KJV)*

The verb phrase "shall receive" does not mean that it is automatic. Jesus gave us further insight into receiving the Holy Spirit operation in our lives:

> *"If ye then, being evil, know how to give good gifts*
> *unto your children: how much more shall your*
> *heavenly Father give the Holy Spirit to them that ask*
> *him?" (Luke 11:13 KJV)*

If we are to receive the Holy Spirit, we must ask. It must be in our heart to allow God to change us into His image and likeness. When the Holy Spirit comes into our life, change must take place. Many today are desiring what they call the finished work of the cross in their lives. The finished work of the cross is the forgiveness of sin. And if that is all that is needed, there would have been no reason for the Day of Pentecost. But Pentecost did come, and the Holy Spirit was given to bring us into a place in God to be born of the Spirit. There is a difference between being baptized in the Holy Spirit and being born of the Spirit. It is only when the work of the Holy Spirit is complete, and the old man is totally destroyed with his old nature and his old way of thinking, that we will be born of the Spirit. When we are born of the Spirit, the Spirit will have complete and total control of our life. Then we, like Jesus, will say, "I only do what I see the Father doing, and I only speak what I hear the Father saying." If we are to enter into the kingdom of God, we must be born of water and the Spirit. Many today, like Nicodemus, only have a carnal understanding of the words of Jesus. Jesus went on to explain to Nicodemus:

> *"That which is born of the flesh is flesh; and that which is born of the Spirit is spirit." (John 3:6 KJV)*

Many today who are claiming to be born again have not yet been born of water. They have failed to deal with the old, Adamic nature and are still servants of sin. Jesus proclaimed, "That which is born of the Spirit is the spirit." Jesus explains what happens to those who are born of the Spirit:

> *"The wind bloweth where it listeth, and thou hearest the sound thereof, but canst not tell whence it cometh, and whither it goeth: so is every one that is born of the Spirit." (John 3:8 KJV)*

When we are born of the Spirit, we become like the wind because we become part of the wind. God can move us by His Spirit. The people will not know where we come from, nor where we are going because man will have lost all hold on our life. We will have become part of Joel's army. God gave Joel a vision of a people who have become like the wind:

Joel's Army

"They shall run like mighty men; they shall climb the wall like men of war; and they shall march every one on his ways, and they shall not break their ranks: Neither shall one thrust another; they shall walk every one in his path: and when they fall upon the sword, they shall not be wounded. They shall run to and fro in the city; they shall run upon the wall, they shall climb up upon the houses; they shall enter in at the windows like a thief. The earth shall quake before them; the heavens shall tremble: the sun and the moon shall be dark, and the stars shall withdraw their shining: And the Lord shall utter his voice before his army: for his camp is very great: for he is strong that executeth his word: for the day of the Lord is great and very terrible; and who can abide it?" (Joel 2:7–11 KJV)

Joel spoke of the day of the Lord, the day of God's judgment. Then he asked, "Who can abide it?" Only those who have been born of water and of the Spirit, those who have become like the wind will be able to abide the day of God's judgment. The prophet Isaiah witnessed this great company of God's army and asked:

"Who area these that fly as a cloud, and as the doves to their windows?" (Isaiah 60:8 KJV)

These are those who are no longer flesh but have become Spirit. These are changed in a moment, in the twinkling of an eye. They have put off being mortals and have put on immortality. They have put off the corrupt body and have put on the incorruptible body. These are those who truly have been born again. These have become the wind of the Lord upon the earth. These will walk into the New Day and inhabit the kingdom for all eternity. These will be the inheritors of the earth who will rule and reign with Christ for one thousand years. These will be joint heirs with Christ.

The winds of the Lord will have completed their work. The east wind will have no effect on Joel's army. God's army will be refreshed by the south wind and empowered by the north wind, bringing deliverance to all God's creation. And the west wind of restoration will have come to restore the earth to its original condition. The earth will be renewed, and God's original plan for man will be fulfilled.

The winds of the Lord are beginning to blow upon the earth. The sealing of God's one hundred and forty-four thousand is about complete. The angels will soon receive the order to release the four winds. We need to ask ourselves, which of the Lord's winds will blow upon us: the east, the north, the south, or the west wind? The wind that will blow upon you will be determined by the way you are walking. Do you need to make an adjustment in your course? Is the wind contrary to you? Or is the wind at your back? Now is the time to change directions if you are walking the wrong way.

God has made us a promise through the prophet Jeremiah:

> *"Behold, the whirlwind of the Lord goeth forth with fury, a continuing whirlwind: it shall fall with pain upon the head of the wicked. The fierce anger of the Lord shall not return, until he hath done it, and until he have performed the intents of his heart: in the latter days ye shall consider it." (Jeremiah 30:23–24 KJV)*

We are truly living in the latter days. It is time to consider the wind before it comes like a whirlwind upon the head of the wicked. God wants to rebuke the contrary wind in His people's lives.

Benefits of the West Wind

1. The west wind saves us from evil.
2. The west wind drives away every calamity facing us.
3. The west wind gives us the power to greatly defeat our enemies in the battle of life.

The Season of New Beginning

The enemy has taken away from us one thing or another. The enemy has deprived us of our joy, happiness, blessing, and favor. We have lost one thing or another to the wicked one. Our lives have been faced with one trial, tribulation, or temptation. But Jesus is going to restore that which was stolen away from us. God is going to restore our lost year and lost blessing. God wants you to have that dream fulfilled. He wants you to have joy. He needs you to possess health in your body. God is a good God! And He has good things in store for us. Don't let the devil steal anything from you, declare restoration over your life, and take what belongs to you. There is a promise of God to restore us to the original position. In effect, after the order of Jonah, anything that has swallowed you—your destiny, your family, your dreams—will vomit you out, and you will gain lost ground in Jesus's name. God knows our pains, the things we have lost in our life: our lost relationships, dreams, past mistakes, lost investments, failed issues, and projects. However, there is an account of how God will restore us in such mighty abundance. You will no longer weep, you will not be ashamed, you will not be disgraced, and you will not be disappointed. God is our restorer, He is ready to restore all our wasted years and put an end to all chronic delays. God knows our need; He is willing to compensate us and give us double for our trouble. Don't just expect one thing because God can give you not just double for your trouble, but can give you triple or multiple to compensate you for time lost, and He will wipe away your years of sorrow, toiling, and waiting.

Areas of Our Life That Will Be Restored

God is going to fully restore everything that we have lost in our life. In the following are the areas where we are going to experience the restoration of our God:

Gain

Losses of many years will be converted into gain. The failures and toiling of many years will be reversed overnight. Peter had been toiling all night without any success, but when the One who can transform failure to success came on board his boat, his failure was reversed and there was restoration within the twinkling of an eye.

Beauty

God has said that He will give you beauty for ashes (Isaiah 61:3). There might be some parts of your life that have been turned to ashes, they are in ruins or destroyed, but God is ready to transform what you think is hopeless into something beautiful and glorious. The ruins and ashes of the past will be converted into the beauty and glory of tomorrow.

Health

God is going to restore your health, restore your body, and restore any malfunctioning cell in your body back to its former state. It is the plan of God that you should prosper and be in good health.

> *"And ye shall serve the LORD your God, and he shall bless thy bread, and thy water; and I will take sickness away from the midst of thee." (Exodus 23:25 KJV)*

Time and life

God will restore to us our wasted time and life. God will restore time and He will restore life. God is a redeemer; He will restore what you think is lost, repackage it, and bring it back to you in a better way.

Looking at Yourself Newly

How do you see yourself? Your self-image is like a photograph that you carry in the wallet of your heart every day of your life. I have noticed that, throughout many years of great men of God ministering to people, most of them do not like themselves very much. God loves you and He wants you to love yourself back. Not in a selfish or self-centered way, but in a healthy and nourishing way. You cannot disclose what you do not have. God loves us and wants us to let that love heal us first before it flows through us then to those around us. If you refuse to receive the love that God has for you by loving yourself properly, then you can never really love others that are around you. Is your opinion of yourself based on your performance? For most of us, that is the case. Our opinion cannot be good because our performance is not consistently good. We are imperfect human beings and we are bound to make mistakes. We want to do things right but we always seem to mess up. That is exactly why we need Jesus. He shows His strength. You are no surprise to God. He knew what you were like when He invited you into a relationship with Himself. He already knows every mistake we will ever make in life, and He loves and desires us anyway. Don't be so hard on yourself. Learn to receive God's mercy on a daily basis. Get up every day and do the best you can for the glory of God who has created you. God already loves you as much as He ever will, and His love for you is just so perfect. At the end of each day, ask God to forgive you for all the sins, mistakes, and wrongs that you have done to Him during the daytime, get a good night's sleep, and start fresh the next day perfectly in our weaknesses.

Satan is against you, however, God is for you. You need to be on God's side and also have faith in Him and His Words because when two agree, they become powerful. You are precious in God's sight, and you have many talents that will be useful to God. Do not just look at everything you think is wrong with you. Do not just look at how far you have to go in life but also look at how far you have come. You are a believer in Jesus Christ now, and that is the beginning of everything wonderful and powerful in your life. It is important for the spiritual growth that you see yourself as having right to stand before God through your faith in Jesus Christ. It is a gift from God. If you always feel bad about yourself, wondering if God is angry at you, you will lose the power that God wants you to walk in. You have authority over the devil as a believer in Jesus, but you must stand before God clothed in righteousness, not the rags of guilt and condemnation. You are free to enjoy yourself now, and it is God's will that you do so and be perfectly fine. Don't base your worth and value on what others say or have said about you in one way or another. Don't base it on how people have treated you or your accomplishments in life. God thought you were valuable enough to send His Son to die for you, and that is a reason to rejoice in. The Bible teaches us perfectly that God wants us to enjoy life, and that will not be possible if you don't enjoy yourself. You are one person you ne'er depart from, not even for one second. If you do not enjoy yourself, you are in for a miserable and an annoying life. Like me, you are probably different from other people that you know, but that is all right. It is actually something God did on purpose. He created us all in a little different way. He likes variety. You are not weird; you are a unique, original, and wonderfully made and you have a greater value than things that are merely copies of something else. Do not compare yourself with others and spend your life competing with them or using other's life to run your own life. Be yourself and enjoy who you are in Christ Jesus. You need to change in those areas that are like the rest of us, and the Holy Spirit will be busy with the rest of your life, working those changes in you. The good news is you are free to enjoy yourself while the work is in progress.

We all know what fear feels like or what it is. It is tormenting and it prevents our progress. Fear will create North American countries shake, sweat, feel weak, and causes them to run from things that they should confront. Fear is not from God. It is Satan's tool to prevent us from living and enjoying the good life God wants us to live. God wants us to live in faith. Faith is the leaning of our entire personalities on God in absolute trust, confidence in His will, His power, wisdom, and goodness. It is the evidence of things that we do not see and the conviction of their reality that we are going to possess them. Faith operates in the spiritual realm. You are probably accustomed to only believing what you can see and feel, but as a child of God, you will need to get comfortable living in the realm of the reality that you cannot see (the spiritual realm). We do not see God because He is a spirit, but we believe firmly in Him and in His Word and promises to us. We don't typically see angels, but God's Word says they are all around us protecting us. By realizing our faith in God and His Word, we can reach into the spiritual realm and pull out things God wants us to enjoy but are not yet a reality. Satan delights in calling our attention to circumstances and trying to make us afraid of the future and getting us lose hope of the good things that the future will bring. On the other hand, God wants us to trust Him, believing that He is greater than any circumstance or threats from the devil. You need to be courageous. Courage isn't the absence of worry, but it is taking action in the presence of it. When God told His servants not to fear, He was not commanding them not to feel fear, but He was telling them to be obedient to Him no matter how they felt. God knows that the spirit of fear will always try to keep us from making progress in our walk with Him. That is why He tells us over and over in His Word that He is with us at all times, and because of that, we do not have to bow down to fear. Only faith pleases God. We receive from God through our faith in Him. Therefore, it is of utmost importance for the new believer in Christ to learn about faith and begin walking in it. Developing robust religion is completely similar to developing robust muscles. You exercise your faith little by little, and each time you do it, you get stronger and better every day. According to your faith in Him, it will be done for you. You may have lived in fear most of your life, but now is the time to exchange that fear for faith in God. It will take time to learn new ways but do not be discouraged or dismayed or give up. Everything in the earth works according to the law of gradual growth. Little by little, everything changes if we keep doing what God tells us to do and keep believing in Him and His Word. God is our real life. In Him, we tend to live and move and have our being. Learning to get pleasure from God can unharness you to get pleasure from each day of your life. You must enjoy fellowship with Him. God is concerned about anything that concerns you, and the Bible actually says that God will perfect what concerns you. Psalms 138: says The Lord will vindicate me; your love Lord, endures forever-do not abandon the works of your hands.

The life you have right now may not be the one you want or that which you desire to end up with, but it is the only one you have at the current time, so you need to start enjoying it. Therefore, you must find the good things in it. Accept the positive and learn to see the good in everything. Enjoy your family and friends. Do not pick them apart and stay busy trying to change them. Pray for them and let God do the changing. Enjoy your work, enjoy your home, and enjoy those ordinary moments of your everyday life. This is possible if you will trust God and decide to have a good attitude. Keep your eyes on God and His Word but not everything that is wrong with you, your life, your family, and the world. God has a good plan for you and He is already starting to work it out. You can rejoice ahead of time, looking forward to the good things to come. Most people live like they believe they cannot enjoy their life as long as they have any kind of problems or situation surrounding them, but that is wrong thinking. Do not dwell on the mistakes or regrets of your past. Continue to think about the greater things that the future holds for you because you have Jesus Christ. You can enjoy whatever you decide to enjoy in your life the way you want. You can enjoy sitting in a traffic jam if you decide to. Remember that I am teaching you a new way of living, and your attitude toward life is a big part of it.

Divine Restoration

Man can restore; man can help because God can use men to help you. However, the help of man can be truncated, but the plan that God has in store for us is greater than what any man can do. Man can help, but something can happen that can truncate help. We see in scriptures that, as a mark of grace, David restored all the lost properties of Saul to Mephibosheth because of the love he had for Mephibosheth's father, Jonathan, Saul's son. However, because Mephibosheth was lame, David instructed Mephibosheth's servant, Ziba, to watch over the properties for Mephibosheth. It happened, however, that during the rebellion of Absalom that temporarily removed David from being king, Ziba cunningly took over the entire possessions and lied to David that Mephibosheth had aligned with Absalom. On David's return to his throne as king, Mephibosheth came back and informed David that Ziba lied to David as to his alignment with Absalom's rebellion, but because Ziba had already taken over his possessions, having hoodwinked David, he didn't mind if Ziba continued to have all his possessions. Mephibosheth, at the end of the day, lost all the inheritance of his father and grandfather, hitherto given to him by David. When God restores, it is permanent.

"I know that whatsoever God doeth, it shall be ever: nothing can be put to it, nor any thing taken from it: and God doeth it, that men should fear before him." (Ecclesiastes 3:14 KJV)

From King Nebuchadnezzar's story, God delivers, He delivers forever, and when He restores, He restores forever, hence no man can stop the plan and purpose of God for your life. Despite the fact that Nebuchadnezzar was in the forest with the beasts for seven years, God preserved his throne till his return and he was fully restored. The fact that you are alive means that God still has a plan for you, and because it is God who has promised restoration, there is something He is still seeing in your life that will not make Him abandon you. Problems can come and the enemy's plan is to destroy you, but thank God for His steady hand upon you because God has the final say.

What happens when god restores?

1. When God restores, joy comes. God declares the end result of a thing from the beginning. Abraham was about to sacrifice his son, Isaac, unto the Lord, but God has seen the level of obedience and love Abraham had for Him had provided a ram locked in a thicket as a substitute. Abraham, in his joy, called the place Jehovah Jireh, which now forms the lyrics of a song, "Jehovah Jireh My Provider."

   "And Abraham called the name of that place Jehovahjireh: as it is said to this day, In the mount of the LORD it shall be seen." (Genesis 22:14 KJV)

2. When God restores, there is always dancing and celebration. Sarah waited on the Lord for a child of her own; she had been

called barren for many years. When God turned her sorrow to laughter, she bore a son and called him Isaac which means laughter (Genesis 21:7). She said, "Who could have thought that He will answer me this way?"

"And she said, Who would have said unto Abraham, that Sarah should have given children suck? For I have born him a son in his old age." (Genesis 21:7 KJV)

3. When God forgave David, He restored his life and his position. God began to use David again to do exploit for Him, and David burst into singing that God had turned his mourning into dancing.

"Thou hast turned on behalf of me my mourning into dancing: M hast postpone my sackcloth, and girded me with gladness" (Psalm 30:11 KJV)

Bringing Glory to God

Everything created by God was created to bring glory to Him. God's glory is that the expression of His goodness and His alternative intrinsic, eternal qualities. We need to bring glory to His name and this can be achieved through the following ways:

Worshipping Him

We bring God glory by worshiping Him. Worship is our first responsibility to God. We worship God by enjoying Him. Worship in a way that is quite laudatory, such as singing and praying to God. Worship could be a modus vivendi of enjoying God, loving Him, and giving ourselves to be used for His functions. When you use your life for God's glory, everything you do can become an act of worship

Loving others

We bring God glory by loving other believers. When you are born once more, you became a part of God's family. Following Christ isn't simply a matter of believing, it additionally includes happiness and learning to like the family of God.

Being like Him

We bring God glory by becoming like Christ. Once we have a tendency to be born into God's family, he wants us to grow to spiritual maturity. What does that look like? Spiritual maturity is changing into the likeness of Jesus of Nazareth within the approach we expect, feel, and act on. When you develop Christ-like character, the more you will bring glory to God. God gave you a replacement life and a replacement nature after you accepted Christ. Now, for the remainder of your life on earth, God wants to continue the process of changing your character.

Giving gifts

We bring God glory by serving others with our gifts. Each person was unambiguously designed by God with abilities, gifts, skills, and abilities. The way you're "wired" is not an accident. God did not offer you your skills for ungenerous functions. They have to profit others, just as others were given abilities for your benefit.

Becoming God's Best Friend

Becoming God's best friend opens to us a lot of favor, blessing, prosperity, and lifting. God deeply desires that we know Him intimately. The ways of becoming God's best friend will thus be examined bellow.

Through constant conversation

You will never grow an in-depth relationship with God by simply attending church once every week or maybe having a daily quiet time. Friendship with God is constructed by sharing all of your life experiences with Him. You can persevere in talking with Him regarding no matter what you're doing or thinking at that moment. He wants to be included in every activity

Through continual meditation

Another way to determine a friendly relationship with God is by brooding about His Word throughout your day. This is called meditation and the Bible repeatedly urges us to meditate on who God is, what He has done, and what He has said. It is impossible to be God's friend except for knowing what He says. You can't love God unless you recognize Him, and you cannot understand Him while not knowing His Word. The Bible says God "revealed himself to Samuel through his word." God still uses that method today. While you cannot spend all day studying the Bible, you can think about it throughout the day, recalling verses you have read or memorized, and mulling them over in your mind. Meditation is commonly misunderstood as some troublesome, mysterious ritual practiced by isolated monks and mystics. But meditation is simply focused on thinking, a skill anyone can learn and use anywhere. When you trust a haul over and over in your mind, that is referred to as worry. When you trust God's Word over and over in your mind, that is meditation. If you recognize a way to worry, you already have the knowledge to meditate. You just have to be compelled to switch your attention from your issues to Bible verses. The more you meditate on God's Word, the less you ought to worry. As a friend of God, God will share His secrets with you if you develop the habit of thinking about His Word throughout the day. God told Ibrahim His secrets, and He did the same with Daniel, Paul, the disciples, and other friends.

Choosing to believe in Him

The first building block of a deeper friendly relationship with God is complete honesty about your faults and your feelings. God does not expect you to be excellent, but He does insist on complete honesty. God allowed Ibrahim to question and challenge Him over the destruction of the town of Sodom. Abraham troubled God over what it'd fancy spare the town, negotiating God down from fifty righteous individuals to solely ten. God patiently listened to David's many accusations of unfairness, betrayal, and abandonment. God didn't murder Jeremiah once he claimed that God had tricked him. Job was allowed to vent his bitterness during his ordeal and in the end.

Bitterness is the greatest barrier to friendly relationship with God. Why would I need to be God's friend if He allowed this? The curative, of course, is to realize that God always act in your best interest, even when it is painful and you don't understand it. But releasing your resentment and revealing your feelings is the first step to healing. We conform God not out of duty, fear, or compulsion, but because we love Him and trust that He knows what is best for us. We want to follow Jesus Christ closely and the closer we follow Him, the deeper our friendship becomes. Great opportunities may come once throughout an extended amount of time, but small opportunities surround us every day. Even through such straightforward acts as telling the truth, being kind, and encouraging others, we bring a smile to God's face. God treasures easy acts of obedience like our quite prayers, praise, or offerings. The more you become God's friend, the more you will care about the things He cares about, grieve over the things He grieves over, and rejoice over the things that bring pleasure to Him. What does God care about most? The redemption of His people. He wants all His lost children found! That's the whole reason Jesus came to earth. The first thing to the heart of God is the death of His Son. The second is that He wants us to share that news with others. To be a devotee of God, you want to care about all the individuals around you whom God cares about. Friends of God tell their friends about God. There is nothing absolutely nothing more vital than developing a friendly relationship with God. It's a relationship that will last forever and through this relationship, you gain lots of things.

Conclusion

In summary, the wind that you will experience will be determined by the way you are walking, and for the west wind to blow upon your life, you need to:

1. Know His voice
2. Listen to His voice
3. Be obedient to His voice

Chapter 6

The Whirlwind

T he whirlwind represents the wind of God's anger and fury. It is the wind of the anger of God at the sin of the wicked one. Through our conduct, we have in one way or another declared war against God. Our carnal mind holds great enmity for God through our daily living. God's only desire is for all sinners to be broken and submit themselves to Him through the salvation of their heart. He desires peace with all men.

> *"For, behold, the Lord will come with fire, and with his chariots like a whirlwind, to render his anger with fury, and his rebuke with flames of fire." (Isaiah 66:15 KJV)*

The whirlwind also represents the power and might of God. God's power is great. God holds the whole oceans in His hand. He created the heaven and the earth. Through His power, we are liberated from the sins that dwell among us. Through His power and might, He made us, made everything on this earth, He parted the Red Sea, and also made the wall of Jericho fall down flat.

> *"The Lord is slow to anger, and great in power, and will not at all acquit the wicked: the Lord hath his way in the whirlwind and in the storm, and the clouds are the dust of his feet." (Nahum 1:3 KJV)*

The whirlwind also sometimes manifests the presence of God.

> *"Then the Lord answered Job out of the whirlwind, and said." (Job 38:1 KJV)*

It also represents the great vengeance of God upon the wicked ones in the earth. The wind shows the wrath of God upon those who perpetrate evils.

> *"God is jealous, and the Lord revengenth; the Lord revengeth, and is furious; the Lord will take vengeance on his adversaries, and he reserveth wrath for his enemies." (Nahum 1:2 KJV)*

The raging whirlwind was used by God to take the prophet Elijah to heaven.

> *"And it came to pass, as they still went on, and talked, that, behold, there appeared a chariot of fire, and horses of fire, and parted them both asunder; and Elijah went up by a whirlwind into heaven." (2 Kings 2:11 KJV)*

Benefits of the Whirlwind

1. Releases the anger of God on the evildoers.

   > *"By the breath of God they perish, And by the blast of His anger they come to an end." (Job 4:9 NASB)*

2. Makes us be broken and to totally submit our life and self to God Almighty.
3. Makes us enjoy the presence of God in things we do and places that we go.

What Is the Presence of God?

The presence of God is His personality (Exodus 33:14).

This is better expressed by the New Living Translation of the Bible, which says "The Lord replied, 'I will personally go with you,

Moses, and I will give you rest—everything will be fine for you." once the presence of God is with us, it implies that He's in person with us. It is really unfortunate these days to hear people praying that one angel or another should be with them or go with them. Moses and the Israelites in the Old Testament era realized that this was not sufficient, so they seriously pleaded that the presence of God would go with them. They knew that, surely, there were many limitations to an angel since he is only a messenger. But God is God, and He is not in any way limited. It is really heartwarming to note that His personality is still with us as Jesus Christ declared, *"I am with always to the end of the age."*

The presence of God is His power (Exodus 33:14).

This truth is expressed by God in the phrase *"I will."* This requires the exertion of power. In fact, I am sure this is paramount in the hearts of Moses and all the people of Israel. They were more interested in the manifestation of the power of God. Really, every time we talk about the presence of God in the Old Testament, it is more of the manifestation of the power of God. This is better seen in the Ark of Covenant, which symbolizes the presence of God. Every time the Ark of Covenant was needed, it was the manifestation of the power of God that the people thirsted for. This power of God manifests in various ways to the blessing of His people. It is wonderful to note that in *Matthew 28:18–20,* we see power and presence related as Jesus Christ declares that all power in heaven and on earth has been given to Him.

The presence of God is His peace (Exodus 33:14).

The Lord told Moses that He would personally go with him and the Israelites and He will give them *rest* and everything will be fine. This is surely a reference to peace. We need to know that the presence of God does not mean the absence of challenges of life. But in the face of these challenges of life, the Lord will give us rest and make everything fine at the conclusion of the whole matter. We are reminded of the presence of the Lord Jesus Christ with the disciples in the boat and how they were attacked by a strong wind. The personality of the Lord in the boat brought about the manifestation of the power of God that led to the peace of mind of the disciples (Mark 4:35–41). It is wonderful to note that Jesus Christ is the Prince of Peace and that His peace is different from the peace of the world. He gives us His peace by His zeal (see Isaiah 9:6–7; John 14:27). We enjoy peace when His Presence is true with us.

The presence of God is the means and end of redemption.

As evangelicals, we talk a lot about the presence of God but seldom look to the Bible to see what it is. When we do, we discover that it's foremost and initially a subject matter on which the story of the Scripture hinges. If we tend to browse our Bibles through, we start to ascertain a twofold pattern. First, the Bible makes clear that the presence of God could be a central goal in God's redemptive mission. All of God's work ends with the Lord abided by man. And second, the presence of God is not only an objective, but it is also the means by which the redemptive mission is fulfilled. God writes Himself into His own story to bring salvation. To understand our Bibles and the way it changes us, we need to know God's presence.

The presence of God finds its greatest expression in Immanuel— God with us.

God Himself comes to save us. Jesus Christ, the Son of God, entered human history to give His life as a ransom for many *(Matthew 20:28; Mark 10:45)*. In His grace, God buys us back in the most unthinkable manner possible: God in Christ became a person, walked among humanity, and died for His folks. In this merciful act, Christ reconciles us to Himself and reopens access to the Father, so that those who were once exiled from His presence might again draw near to God.

How to Attract the Presence of God

Humility

The first principle is the importance of humbling ourselves before the Lord. Humility attracts God's presence like nothing else. We see this in so many passages in both the Old and New Testaments. For example, in 1 Kings 21, when the prophet Elijah came and pronounced judgment on Ahab, an extraordinarily wicked man, Ahab humbled himself with fasting. And what did God do? He relented and put off judgment to the next generation. Often in the Scriptures, the words "humbling" and "fasting" go together. Fasting is important as a means through which we humble ourselves. There is no question that we are to fast. Jesus in the Sermon on the Mount talks about what you are to do when you fast. Fasting was a practice of the church from the earliest of times. God's people fasted. The apostles fasted. And if the apostles needed to fast to help humble themselves, and if Nehemiah in his day needed this, and if Ezra needed this, and if Moses needed this, then surely we do all need this.

Only desperate people will deny themselves. The self-righteous will not humble their souls. Neither will the self-satisfied or self-indulgent employ this discipline. But deep religious hunger will cause folks to become therefore desperate that they humble their souls by abstinence. I know of churches that have called on their people to fast from food, television, and computers for the expressed purpose of diligently seeking God. Pastors have, from time to time, led their congregations into seasons of ruefulness and brokenness before God. These congregations were in dead earnest about the condition of their souls. They longed to have Jesus of Nazareth back in their interior. They realized that no price is too high to pay for a divine visitation. I know of two quarreling churches that took out a full-page newspaper ad to ask the community to forgive them for their poor testimony

The Word of God

A second principle for attracting the presence of God is taking in massive amounts of the Scripture through reading and through preaching and teaching. Knowing the Scripture is extraordinarily important. Without knowledge of the Scripture, it is impossible to know the heart of God. An amazing incident happened at Princeton in the early 1800s. The president at that time, Ashbel Green, noticed godlessness among the students because of the influence of the enlightenment. He therefore issued a decree that students were required to memorize five chapters of the Bible per week. Can you imagine what happened? In a matter of a few weeks, there were massive conversions, massive changes in people's lives. How can you have the precepts of the Holy Scriptures coursing through your mind that much without being radically changed by them?

In American culture, we are arrogant and think we are so much smarter now. But the people who have come before us were brilliant people and they dedicated themselves profoundly to the Word of God. For example, William Wilberforce, who led the charge to outlaw the slave trade in the British Empire, on the way home from Parliament, would recite from memory the 176 verses from Psalm 119. Another example is Saint Patrick who was taken as a slave to Ireland, and to pass the time as a shepherd would recite from memory fifty psalms— as a teenager. It is no surprise that once he escaped, the Lord used him to go back to Ireland to lead much of the nation to Christ.

Repentance

A third principle is a repentance, giving Christ lordship in all matters. Many Christians are waiting for something to happen when instead they should be getting on their knees. In the example I gave earlier about King Asa, the first thing he did was to tell the people to take courage and put away their detestable idols. They took action. Let's face it! In America, there are enough Christians that if we were really upset about our national sins, they would be quickly gone. But we do not take them to heart. We do not take action. In our own lives, we have many things that keep us from living righteously, from being repentant, from putting Christ first, and from calling others—even non-Christians—to holiness. God wants us to repent and make Christ Lord, then He will send His Spirit on us.

Over again in Israel's history, the people were faithful to keep regular times of prayer and fasting, yet were rebellious against God. This hypocrisy enraged God and He reproved them in *Joel 2:12–13 NASB: "'Yet even now,' declares the LORD, 'Return to Me with all your heart, and with fasting, weeping and mourning; and rend your heart and not your garments.' No return to the LORD your God, for*

He is gracious and compassionate, slow to anger, abounding in lovingkindness, and relenting of evil."

Obedience and holiness

The fourth principle is ongoing obedience and holiness in our lives and the righteousness that comes with that. We have enormous sway with God when we live consistently righteous lives. There is so much emphasis on the imputed righteousness that comes from Christ, which is absolutely true, that we forget that there is also sanctification righteousness that is vital. We know this implicitly. When you have a prayer concern, a burden on your heart, do you ask a Christian who is living a so-so life to pray for you, or do you ask a devout follower of Christ who has walked faithfully with Him for years? You know in your spirit that the devout follower has more sway with God because of their consistent and righteous walk with Him.

We see this in the Old Testament. Sometimes God would be so angry with the people of Israel, He would say, "Even if Moses were here and prayed for you, I would not do it." We know at times that Moses, because of his righteousness and sway with God, prevented a judgment against the people. And who knows if some reading this may have such righteousness before the Lord that your praying is keeping back all sorts of judgments that could be coming on this nation. We must constantly be teaching this and living this kind of consistent righteousness so that we have all the more sway with God. He hears, He bends His ear all the more closely to hear from us if we live a righteous life. Now let me say that we do not control God. He is sovereign over all people and nations, and He does whatever He wants. But He has made it clear what He delights in and what has sway with Him and what moves Him. And we ignore this to our own peril.

Perseverance

A fifth principle is perseverance. We cannot seek God just for a weekend or a month and think we are going to see radical changes. We need to seek God as a lifestyle. As I read earlier from *Psalm 105:3–4,* we are to seek the face of the Lord "continually." We must seek Him constantly as a way of life. We must constantly be putting in the energy and the work to draw close to Him. Many people will get stirred up, encouraged, and inspired by something for a short season. They will put evil out of their lives and start praying more, but then they lose hope after a week or two. Part of the problem is that our American culture has such an instantaneous mindset. As one author of the history of American revivals shared in effect with me, "We think things are going to happen immediately, that is if we just say it once then we just need to have faith and it will happen if God is interested." But this is not the model in the Scripture, and it is not the model we see in church history. Instead, people sought after God for days, weeks, years. Evan Roberts, for example, spent years reading the Bible and praying every day for hours and hours, and then the Lord anointed him and used him in the Welsh Revival in 1904. We need to commit ourselves to live like this, and as we do, there will be periodic outpourings of the Spirit with wonderful happenings to the glory of God. Sometimes it is going to be hard, but we must persevere day in and day out, week after week, year after year. We must persevere in doing what is right before the Lord in seeking His face, praying, fasting, and repenting. We need to keep going and encourage other believers to keep going. Anything worth having in this life requires perseverance and diligence. It is no different from the Lord. We need to have perseverance in seeking after Him.

It is extraordinary to note the toil and diligence that some apply to numerous aspects of their lives, be it education, athletics or a hobby. In season and out of season, many Christians faithfully and diligently work hard to be better educated or skilled in athletics or a musical instrument. However, several of those same Christians exhibit terribly low prioritization of their walk with the Nazarene, and would be so surprise why they do not have the Lord's presence and power in their lives. Those who are out of shape physically usually know why they are out of shape—they don't exercise enough. Those who don't perform well on their tests recognize that always the explanation is that they did not study. Yet, several Christians have very little conclusion and power in their lives and that they honestly don't have any idea why. They have not been praying and reading the Scripture diligently, fasting, humbling themselves, repenting their sins, and practicing consistent obedience to God. God is displeased with them and perhaps even opposing them, and yet they are completely ignorant of it.

Gathering others

The sixth principle is what I call gathering others. There are two parts to this: the gathering with others and the gathering of others. Regarding the gathering of others, I am going to read Zechariah 8:20–23. This passage is what Jonathan Edwards said was the most descriptive passage of revival in the Bible. "Thus says the Lord of hosts: Peoples shall nevertheless come back, even the inhabitants of many cities. The inhabitants of one town shall attend another, saying, 'Let us go at once to entreat the favor of the Lord and to seek the Lord of hosts; I myself am going.' Many peoples and strong nations shall come to seek the Lord of hosts in Jerusalem and to entreat the favor of the Lord. Thus says the Lord of hosts: In those days ten men from the nations of each tongue shall take hold of the gown of a person, saying, 'Let us go with you, for we've detected that God is with you.'"

What you see happening here is that as we are seeking the Lord and gathering other people to join us in seeking the Lord, He works supernaturally in people we have not even talked to, giving them an eagerness. We have heard the amazing stories of what God has done in revivals, such as during the Businessmen's Revival in the 1800s when even before people arrived in New York City, the Spirit came on them and they came to faith in Christ. We see similar things on our campus. Being an evangelical Christian on such campuses is not popular. These environments have a lot of suspicion and stereotypes of Christians, but as we have been diligently seeking the Lord, students that have not been involved nor met anyone in our organization will contact us and say that they feel like they need God and want to meet with someone to learn more about what this means. This is not our clever strategy or programs, but this is God working in their hearts and in their minds so that the Spirit is calling them to Himself. The second part is gathering with others. God intends for us to be vibrant and devoted to Him, and one of the patterns and means for this is having our own regular, daily times with the Lord. But we should also set aside multiple days yearly when we spend time with other believers to be encouraged and strengthened in our faith. These times should include Bible teaching, prayer, confession of sin, encouragement, and worship

The Old Testament provides a pattern. Every year, there were three feasts at which all the Jewish males were required to be in solemn assembly. One was for a whole week—the Feast of Unleavened Bread. One was for a day—the Day of Pentecost. The other was for another week—the Feast of Booths. What happened during these times was extraordinary. In one such an account (Nehemiah 8:1–8), the people gathered and Ezra read to them from the book of the law for about six hours. Another gathering is recorded in 2 Chronicles 30, and when the people left, they went through villages destroying altars and idols because they were stirred up by the Spirit of God. God knew the people needed these regular times in order to be vibrant and devoted to Him. We need special times to be renewed, encouraged, strengthened, and taught all that the Lord would have us to be. A recent book reports that in American history, many people used "vacation" to go camping meetings to spend a whole week praising and seeking the Lord, and incredible things happened. There was no other vacation. Now we have secularized our vacation times and think we need to get away and we need to rest. We forget that the Lord is our rest. There is no greater rejuvenation than when we are in the presence of the Lord.

Prayer

The seventh principle is prayer. A couple of years ago, I asked our staff how much time a student would need to spend with the Lord each day in Bible reading and prayer if he/she wanted to be like Daniel, a person in an influential position to make an impact for Christ. What if this student wanted to have the same spiritual depth and walk with the Lord as Daniel had, so that when presented with similar challenges, this person would not just fold up but have a vibrant witness for Christ? It seems no one wants to answer this question. But if that same student went to a track coach and asked what amount of time is required to compete at the collegiate level, the track coach would know and would not hesitate to tell what it takes. Finally, people came forward and most of them said two or three hours a day of Bible reading and prayer was needed. As a result of this, our staff significantly increased our own times with the Lord. To get the amount I wanted, I decided to set aside time with Him in the morning and some at night. I love the spiritual impact dividing the time had on my life. The Scripture often talk about spending time with the Lord night and day *(e.g. Psalm 1:2; Daniel 6:10; Deuteronomy 6:7; Luke 18:7; 1 Timothy 5:5)*, and I find it helpful to have set times in the morning and at night, if not also in the middle of the day, to cry out to the Lord.

From the best—we can reconstruct—believers in the first century spent from an hour and a half to three hours in Scripture reading and prayer over the course of each day. This is radical for Americans because we, American Christians, have become lovers of pleasure. I say that with a heavy heart and not with a judgmental spirit. We have time for many things...Facebook, television, sports, hobbies, and so on, but not the time to seek the Lord for an hour and a half to three hours a day. The time is there, but we have become lovers of pleasure. We need to have a radical change. You may say, "I cannot pray this long. How do I do this?" This is something you can grow into. There may be times that are difficult and you must arouse yourself to pray. But there are other times when it is absolutely glorious and you sense the Spirit of God upon you, which is the way and the life God intends for us. Sometimes we pray on our own and at other times, corporately. This is all part of what it is to seek the Lord diligently. It will take work and effort and it will be hard and you will need other people, but it will be glorious and wonderful. God has given our country an extraordinary spiritual heritage as few countries have on earth. His destiny and purposes for this country are not yet fulfilled, and it is up to us to press in with our whole hearts and seek Him diligently. *"Dear Lord, give me diligence and perseverance in seeking Your face. Give me the energy to get up and pray in the mornings and to pray at night. Do not let me become calloused. Do not let me have a spirit of unbelief. Lord, give me the self-control to fast the times I need to fast and to repent of sins and to call others to seek You. Let me have faith, Father, and call many, many thousands in the United States to have the same attitude and heart. Lord, we need many more to seek*

Your face so that You will hear and respond. We believe that when we draw near to You, You will draw near to us."

Giving

In Acts 10, Cornelius was also a generous giver. It was the combination of His prayer life and giving that became a memorial before God attracting His presence. Your giving, when combined with prayer, will catch God's attention. Not only did Cornelius receive the Holy Spirit, but so did his entire family and ultimately the entire Gentile race. It was one of the most significant outpourings of God in history, all triggered through prayer and giving. You can attract God's presence to your own life through giving furthermore. You can live a life saturated with the glory of God. I share about these eight keys and so much more in my brand new teaching set "Shift Your Atmosphere, Transform Your Life." I encourage you to invest in your next level of spiritual breakthrough. The four teachings include "Shift Your Atmosphere, Eight Keys to Attracting the Glory," "Create a Space for God to Fill," and "Secrets to Building a Glory Habitation."

Unity

Where there is unity, God commands a blessing. When we come into unity with other believers we form a corporate habitation in which God can fill. In 2 Chronicles 5, as the worshippers made one sound to the Lord, they attracted the presence of God to the point where the glory became so strong no one could remain standing. The temple was filled with glory. As you keep unified with God and different believers you may attract God's glory.

Magnifying God's true nature

This is one of the most important keys and one we must learn more about. There is something glorious that happens when we get a revelation of the true nature of God and choose to magnify and exalt those attributes of God in worship. In 2 Chronicles 5, the priests used very specific wording in their worship. They magnified very specific attributes of God's nature. It is this specific style of worship that draws

God's glory. They specifically magnified His goodness, mercy, and loving-kindness. As they did the temple was filled with glory. I share additional facts concerning this in my teaching set, "Shift Your Atmosphere." There were reasons why this specific worship attracted the glory.

Obedience

The flip side to repentance is obedience, and authentic repentance always leads to obedience. Repentance involves recognizing that you have thought wrongly in the past and determining to think aright in the future, acknowledging what has to be brought before God. Obedience is daily walking in sanctity and surrender to the Nazarene as Lord. God delights and draws close to those who live righteous lives. Every culture has characteristics that reinforces and commends the eternal commands of God and yet also has values that are contrary to the will of God, which need to be brought into alignment with Him. American culture within the twenty first century has a lot of going for it, including a strong value on racial tolerance, faithful stewardship of the environment, and caring for the poor. It doesn't mean that all of these social conditions are as they should be, but in general, society values what God values in these areas. On the opposite hand, there are current American values that stand in stark contrast to the ways of God, and it is the duty of Christians to faithfully reject cultural norms and adopt God's values. Faithfully walking with God even when this bring one in conflict with the encircling culture exemplifies a righteous and holy life, and God loves the righteous and draws close to them.

In the class of sexual integrity, American culture has strayed far away from the biblical norms it once embraced. Fornication, pornography, homosexuality, adultery, and divorce are all common in Christian as well as non-Christian culture in the United States, greatly grieving the heart of God. Much of this sexual immorality results in abortion, which has claimed tens of millions of lives in the last fifty years amounting to a holocaust worse than the holocaust of World War II, and even worse than the era of slavery in the United States. God forgives once there's real remorse, and America and American Christians have much to repent over in this area. Another Yankee cultural norm that grieves the guts of God is materialism and greed. Although America is the richest country in the history of the world, the average American only gives away 2% of his income, and Christians are only slightly better at about 3.5%. Giving away 100% of financial gain was the norm for pious Jews and Christians within the initial century, such that a person was considered generous only if he gave considerably more than 10%. Now, it's thought to be exceptional if Christians disclose simply 100%. How has our thinking altered that we have a tendency to be stingy at a time? Every Christian should become independent from this wicked defense and learn to measure liberally. Test your experiences to discern whether or not they are truly encounters with God. It's necessary to ask the Holy Ghost to help you valuate personal experiences that will bring you into contact with God's manifest presence, rather than simply assuming that an exhilarating religious expertise extremely originates with God. To recognize if a selected expertise is really from God, ask: ***"Does it have clear, telltale marks of being from the God whose nature the Bible reveals?" "Is it in line with biblical principles?"***

Walking in the glory

> *"But we all, with unveiled face, beholding as in a mirror the glory of the Lord, are being transformed into the same image from glory to glory, just as by the Spirit of the Lord." (2 Corinthians 3:18 NKJV)*

The glory of God appears in an abode. The original house for the glory of God was the tabernacle. But beneath the New Covenant, the Holy Spirit builds a temple in every believer. ***First Corinthians 3:16 says, "Do you not know that you are the temple of God and that the Spirit of God dwells in you?"*** We are God's house—His temple. Only, this temple is not any longer during a fastened location. This house will walk and speak and preach the gospel. Now, it's one thing to have the glory, but it's another to know how to walk in it. The good news? You have everything you wish within you to try to therefore. When the believers told the glory of God at Pentecost, they didn't just go back to living normal lives. They emerged from that place as separate from the rest of the world and as light in the midst of darkness. They went out and began turning the planet the wrong way up for Logos. They preached the gospel and worked miracles, signs, and wonders; and therefore the Lord added to the Church daily those who were being saved *(Acts 2:47)*. That's the glory we'd like to be in operation in!

The early Christians were no different from Christians today. But here's the key: Those first believers received the same Spirit you did when you got saved and baptized with the Holy Ghost. When you come in the glory of God, you have a fire in you that the devil cannot withstand.

The Power of the Presence of God

God's presence is with us wherever we go. God made covenants to us to show that He wanted to be present with humanity. He gave us the law to show people how to conduct themselves in His presence. And He established sacrifices once sin separated folks from His presence. So much of what we have a tendency to see within the Old Testament relates on to the presence of God. One of the foremost fascinating options of the Old Testament law was a tent, referred to as the tabernacle. This was where God would meet with His people. God had been leading Israel through the desert as a pillar of cloud by day and a pillar of fire by night. With the tabernacle, God was making a home for Himself on earth. The tabernacle would go with Israel wherever they go. In the Garden of Eden, Adam and Eve could interact with God without the division that comes through sin. They lived in peace with God, His creation, and one another. The distance we have a tendency to feel from God currently wasn't a region of the human expertise before the autumn. The sins of Adam and Eve made our fellowship with God to be destroyed. First, Adam and Eve broke the relationship by sinning, and then they tried to hide from God's presence when He entered the garden.

The tabernacle was God creating a way for His presence to dwell on earth in the midst of His people. Because the laws governing the tabernacle, its design, and the ceremonies involved are so complex, it is easy to miss the significance of the tabernacle as we read the Old Testament. The gorgeous truth was that God yet again blessed His individuals with the best gift He may give Himself. From the moment that the Holy Spirit filled the early church, God's presence has dwelt on earth through His Church. But when Jesus returns to set the world to right, the whole world will be filled with God's presence. What Adam and Eve enjoyed in Eden are knowledge on each purpose on the world as revived humanity enjoys God's revived presence in an exceedingly revived creation. God is holy. He is all powerful. We should not take His presence for granted. It is solely through the cross and the resurrection of Logos that the way into His presence, and also the gift of the Holy Spirit living at intervals, you are formed potential. The Father incorporates a secret place for all that He wishes to dwell in with us. Since neither time nor house restricts God's presence, the presence-filled secret place that He has for us is accessible anytime, anywhere. It is a place where we can spend quality time with Him even in the midst of the frenzied world around us. God is spirit and solely the spirit of man will grasp Him extremely. In the deep spirit of a person, the fire must glow or his love is not the true love of God. The great dominion are people who admired God over others. Living a Holy life is an eloquent testimony that one is well aware of the presence of God. How can you indulge in sinful behavior when you know that God is there with you and sees and knows everything you do? It is not possible. It is because you are not conscious of His presence. Moses was convinced that while God's presence was not in his life, it had been useless for him to try something. When he spoke face to face with the Lord, he stated boldly, "If thy presence goes not with me, carry us not up hence" (Exodus 33:15). He was an expression, ***"Lord, if you're not with us, we're not going to make it. We won't take one step unless we have a tendency to assured of your presence."*** Moses knew it had been God's presence among them that set them excluding all different nations. The same is true of God's people today. The only thing that sets us apart from nonbelievers is God's presence with us, leading us, guiding us, working His will in and through us. His presence drives out fear and confusion. The only manner for the United States to be guided or ruled is to do battle and survive in these times, and to have God's presence with them. When His presence is in our interior, nobody will destroy the United States. But without Him we are helpless, reduced to nothing. Let all the nations of the planet trust in their mighty armies, iron chariots, and practiced troopers. We will trust within the manifest presence of the Lord. With God's presence lasting in you, you'll be able to bear any fireplace, and you won't just survive but will be kept and protected through it all. When God's Spirit is, a gift, with the United States, we can be strong and courageous because we trust His promise to go with us in all our ways.

Releasing the Presence of God

One of our greatest responsibilities to God and people is to pursue or provide more eloquent displays of the gospel, or even miracles. Neither is it merely to speak the truth in the sense of preaching or a one-on-one witness of the gospel. Our responsibility is to grasp God and acknowledge Him as the Creator. Learning how to do this effectively should capture our hearts and attention for a lifetime. God is a God of the covenant. He is confident enough and sovereign enough to bind Himself to agreements with His children. Being obedient to God releases upon us the presence of God, His power and His glory cannot be properly or even accurately represented without power. Miracles are completely necessary for folks to check Him clearly. Testifying about these miracles is part of the debt that we owe the world. When we speak, He comes to confirm what was spoken. God has chosen to reveal Himself through people who yield to Him. His appearances are often spectacular and dramatic, as seen throughout history. His manifestations through His people may at times be similarly amazing, yet are often practical and normal.

We must focus on God's heart for the nations. The testimony and the prophetic anointing it releases will bring about a return of the nations to God's ordained purposes. This is the reason He has given us everything as an inheritance. We need everything to accomplish our assignment. Our greatest treasure is God Himself. Our greatest privilege is to manifest Him. The people of God around the world are crying out for God to show up in a more important way. God will allow us to carry as much of His presence as we're willing to jealously guard. It has never crossed our minds how much is available to us now. The record of God's activities among men is not to be hidden or forgotten.

God's Presence in the Lives of the Bible Characters

Isaiah

God told Isaiah of a special promise he makes to those he loves: "Fear not: for I have redeemed thee, I have called thee by thy name; thou art mine. When thou passest through the waters, I will be with thee; and through the rivers, they shall not overflow thee: when thou walkest through the fire, thou shalt not be burned; neither shall the flame kindle upon thee. For I am the Lord thy God…and I have loved thee…" Isaiah 43:1–5 KJV.

Gideon

The Lord told Gideon that "The Lord is with thee, thou mighty man of valour…. Go in this thy might, and thou shalt save Israel…" (Judges 6:12, 14 KJV). Although Gideon thought of himself a coward, God calls him a "mighty man of valour."

Joshua

God secured Joshua that no enemy might stand against him once His presence was with him: "There shall not any man be able to stand before thee all the days of thy life: as I was with Moses, thus I will be with thee, I will not fail thee, nor forsake thee" (Joshua 1:5 KJV). Be strong and of good courage.

Abraham

God's presence was also evident in Abraham's life, even the heathen around him recognized the difference between their lives, and Abimelech confirmed the presence of God in the life of Abraham saying, "God is with thee in all that thou doest" (Genesis 21:22 KJV).

Abimelech also noticed that there is something different in the life of Abraham. God is with you wherever you go.

The Power of His Presence

His presence reveals our secret sins

The light of God's presence reveals the dark places in our hearts. The longer we have a tendency to pray in God's presence, the more the sunshine shines and highlights our sin. Through the awing power of God's presence, He became more and more aware of the light shining in His heart. God's everlasting nature is a component of *who* He is. For us, aliveness isn't automatic or natural. It is a gift from the everlasting God.

His presence comes through the facility of the Holy Spirit

The presence of God radically changes our lives and the lives of others around us. He gives power to both our words and our actions. He makes possible signs and miracles. This is what characterized the early church. The coming of the Holy Spirit on the day of Pentecost brought a great outpouring of the presence of God. God is present among His people now by the Holy Spirit. He is present within our community and society.

His presence requires respect

God's presence lives within us. Let not take His presence for granted because His Spirit which lives in us makes us enjoy His presence. God's presence brought a great blessing to David. David had great respect and reverence for God and His presence and as a result of this, the household of David was blessed. He often asked for God's steering concerning what he ought to do.

The Benefits of the Presence of God

Favor

The presence of God guarantees us the favor of God. Through the way God favors us, people will be aware that we have the presence of God with us. Favor is evidence of God's presence. Favor means God will single you out, God will prefer you, God will endorse you. It also means God will unduly love you; He will indulge you. Through the favor of God with us, what God will take from others, He will not take from us.

Distinguish

To distinguish means to be different, to set apart, to be special, to be singled out, to be marked out, to excel, to bring fame and honor. When God's presence is with you, it distinguishes you and you will be the apple of God's eye, you will not make a mistake, and you will stand out and be fulfilled in that which you do.

Victory

God's presence guarantees all-around victory. When God's presence is with you, no man will be able to stand before you, and no man will conquer you. Everything you lay your hands on shall prosper when God is with you. The presence of God with you makes him go ahead of you and through it, nothing will limit you. When people fight with you, they will not prevail because God is with you, and when you go through challenges, God will be with you to deliver you.

Rest

God's presence gives you rest. Rest means the absence of struggle. The presence of God makes you ride on the eagle's wing and calm for you every area of your toiling and struggling.

Prosperity

God's presence makes you prosper in all your ways. *"**The keeper of the jail looked to not something that was beneath his hand; as a**"* *result of the LORD was with him, and that which he did, the LORD made it prosper" (Genesis 39:23 paraphrased).* Joseph prospered even in jail due to the presence of God.

Ways of Invoking the Presence of God

Surrender

We need to surrender our lives to Jesus Christ because God's presence cannot abide where there is a sin. Living in sin does not allow the Holy Spirit to dwell in us. God's presence is not only about God walking beside you, but dwelling in you to cause you to do His will.

> *"Then I will give them one heart, and I will put a new spirit within them, and take the stony heart out of their flesh, and give them a heart of flesh, that they may walk in My statutes and keep My judgments and do them; and they shall be My people, and I will be their God." (Ezekiel 11:19–20 NKJV)*

Praise Him

Praising God causes you to experience the supernatural. Paul and Silas were praying and praising God, and suddenly, there was a great earthquake that the very foundations of the prison were shaken, and at once, all the doors were opened and everyone's shackles were loosened. Praising God opens the door of extraordinary things.

Giving offering

Giving to God makes the presence of God abide with you. Solomon gave a thousand burnt offerings and that same night, God appeared before him. If you have been experiencing the presence of God, stay close to Him. If you forsake God, He will forsake you, and if you don't forsake God, He won't forsake you.

Conclusion

In conclusion, the whirlwind releases the great anger of God on those perpetrating evil. It totally brings them to end in their own evil way. My questions are, "Are you an associate evildoer? Do you got those around you?" I would greatly advise us to turn now and turn back to God to forgive us of all our evil doings so that His whirlwind of anger would not be released upon us.

Chapter 7

The Boisterous Wind: The Noisy Wind

The boisterous wind represents a noisy and energetic wind. So severe in nature. Peter, an apostle of Christ, experiences this noisy wind:

> *"So He said, "Come." And when Peter had come down out of the boat, he walked on the water to go to Jesus. But when he saw that the wind was boisterous, he was afraid; and beginning to sink he cried out, saying, "Lord, save me!" (Matthew 14:29–30 NKJV)*

The wind instills the fear that we cannot do it, neither can we achieve good success from that which we do. It rendered us powerless in that situation that we are facing. As a businessman whose business is failing, it makes you believe that your business cannot grow again whereas it can through the help of God Almighty if you invite Him to come and take control of it. As a sick person, it instills in you the thought that you cannot be cured of such sickness whereas you can be cured by the power that is in the name of Jesus. The wind is a threatening wind. It inflicts on us fear which makes you forget that you have God as a backing

The boisterous wind causes mankind generally a lot of troubles ranging from diseases, calamity, or suffering from God:

> *"Then the Lord will strike you with wasting disease, with fever and inflammation, with scorching heat and drought, with blight and mildew, which will plague you until you perish." (Deuteronomy 28:22 NIV)*

Overcoming the Fear and Stopping the Doubt

Self-doubt will hurt you both personally and professionally, making you feel inadequate, overwhelmed, and insecure when it creeps in. But the all-time low line is that it's your own personal battle. Self-doubt will cause you to sabotage your possibilities at success. Self-doubt cans seriously impair your performance at work. When you experience bad self-doubt, you simply do not do the things you need to do, and you are scared to try new activities, and lose the motivation to perform. It prompts defensive actions to avoid failure which will limit your growth. Self-doubt may be a worrying and persuasive voice that holds you back. It holds you back from seizing your opportunities. It makes obtaining what you started or finishing things more difficult than they have to be. Self-doubts are most often just monsters in our head that our mind may use to keep us from making changes and to keep us within the comfort zone. Self-doubt and fear destroy lives.

Fear is the link with a lack of both faith and fear of the Lord. When wearing fear, we tend to not seem to be trusting God and sometimes, fearing something or someone other than God! Fear is a weapon that the enemy uses to torment us and to dictate feelings and behavior to us. God desires to deliver everybody *who* struggles with worry. When God's individuals are free from worry, they can walk in power, authority, and victory. Multiple fears begin with the lies that the enemy has told us, which shows why the devil is called the "father of lies." He tries to handicap us with fear as a result of his awareness that, in reality, each can set and build the North American nations free. The devil is the natural feeling of worry against the North American nations to make us feel helpless in resisting him. He wants us to doubt the Lord and ourselves because it makes him appear stronger than he really is. The devil discredits God in each approach he does, whispering lying accusations to us about God, as he did to Adam and Eve. Fears are real feelings that you cannot deny. All of us have felt one bad omen in our stomachs at one time—the nervousness that comes when we may have to give a speech or compete in an event, or public speaking. The adrenaline our bodies produce helps us deal with stressful situations, but it also makes us feel sick. But this is often a form of fine worry that helps the North American nations be more alert and to perform higher. A key to overcoming fear is to find the root of where it began. If you're suffering from worry, ask the Holy Spirit to show you the root cause. Get utterly alone with God for a time of material possession and He will search your entire life for any and each worry. Fear will become a defense in our lives after we experience trauma. Being in an accident, witnessing violence, or having other traumatic experiences can make us vulnerable to the spirit of fear. For example, Sue had been bitten by two dogs as a child, so naturally, she was afraid of dogs as she grew up. She then begged God to heal that memory and to free her from that worry.

Keys to Overcoming Fear

Thank God for His love

God is caring and devoted to respond to our prayers. In this life, we face many troubles, sickness, opposition, temptation, exhaustion, trials, and attacks. God, in His love and faithfulness, preserves us. God is ever faithful towards us in everything we do. Even at the time when we sin against Him, God still preserves us and keeps us safe because He does not want the death of a sinner but the repentance of a sinner. The Lord will fulfill His purpose over our lives, therefore, we need to thank Him.

Live in the love of God

Love is the counter poison to worry; perfect love drives out fear. God's perfect love turns fear out to the doors and expels every trace of terror. Love is the opposite of fear. They are like oil and water. Love is something everyone wants. Fear is something everybody wants to get rid of. The more you're keen on Him and demonstrate that reality by caring for each other, the less you will fall prey to worry. Develop a culture of love giving and receiving love.

Stand firm in the love of God

People who know their God are people of love. Love is not weak. Those who understand God resist evil leaders. Stand firm in your faith in God in the midst of all evil or circumstances. Thank God for His love, live in the love of God, overcome your fears, stand firm, and resist evil.

Stay in the Word

A pilot has to log a certain number of flight hours per month in order to maintain proficiency. If not, then they're not considered to be "current." As a believer, you need to stay in God's Word to keep your faith built up. Do go out of His Word. Do not do things out of His Word but instead do it in and through the Word of God and you will see that you will greatly overcome the fear.

Associations

Your association determines who you are. Your main friends need to be people who are in positive faith as you are. You must find people who inspire you and encourage you to live for God and trust His Word. Don't let wrong associations pull you down and drain your religion. Do not mingle with the wrong individual who will instill in you the fear of the unknown.

Take action

There comes a point where prayer time is over. Ask God to show you what you can do right now (even without money) to get started. Ask for His wisdom. You can do research, look at homes, make phone calls, etc. There's something that you can do to get started that requires either zero money or little money. You must exercise discipline and be committed to your task and God can reward you.

The Force of Fear

There are two forces that you will deal with throughout our life. They are the force of fear and the power of faith. In my own words, fear is the opposite of faith and faith is the confidence in God's ability that says you can do it even when others assume that you cannot.

"And deliver them who through fear of death were all their lifetime subject to bondage." (Hebrews 2:15 KJV)

In the above verse, I would like us to note that first and foremost, that fear connects us to bondage in life. In other words, when you allow fear to rule your life, it puts limitations on your life and also keeps you in bondage. Fear is like a prison with high walls that will try to keep you locked up even till eternity. When you allow fear to have the upper hand in something, then you are missing out on what you could have had by faith. Fear says, "You can't do this," whereas faith says, *"You can do all things through Christ who strengthens you" (Philippians 4:13 paraphrased)*.

Secondly, the verse above identifies that the ultimate fear known to mankind is the fear of death. Perhaps you have never thought of it this way, but death is the greatest enemy that you will ever face in this life. The root of each concern may be a sense of danger or loss—and death is actually the final word, loss. Yet in the Bible, it says that we have been delivered from death through the resurrection of Jesus Christ! The resurrection of Christ is our foundation for expecting "victory" instead of "loss." If so, that we have been delivered from the ultimate loss, then why anything should intimidate us? Why should we be bothered about death? Once we begin to understand just how complete and awesome our victory is in Christ, it will be a great step forward in our mind and heart for overcoming fear. You need to make a decision that you will never again let fear hold you back from God's best. Whether you are learning how to fly airplanes, buying a home, traveling to other nations for missionary work, or whatever, do not be afraid. In your life, it may be an entirely different area where you need to apply this key. It may be the worry of beginning a family, shopping for an automobile, being a missionary, or launching a brand new project. Whatever the case, God needs you to beat the force of concern and trust in His power and His ability to figure things out on your behalf. He wants you to fly like an eagle.

Please Be Anywhere But Not Hell

The Bible speaks about hell much more than heaven. It is probably because more people will end up in hell than in heaven. In the Bible, the person who mentions the most about hell is Jesus. Obviously, Jesus knew about hell more than any other person. Nowadays, many preachers commit the sin of being silent about hell. They do not preach about hell because people do not like to hear those sermons. What do you think will bring the most severe suffering in the world to a person? I believe it is fire. The most fearful injury is a burn. Its cure is most painful. Hell is a place full of fire. Many Christians are convinced that they will go to heaven because they have faith in Jesus, but I want to ask them, "Have you repented of your sins?" Faith without repentance is false faith, which will not rescue us from hell. Repentance is not merely regretting and confessing your sins, but cutting off your sins. At the same time, repentance is cutting off "all your offenses." There are two kinds of people. One kind consists of those in Christ who have repented; while the second kind consists of those outside His fold who have not repented. In other words, one group of people will go to heaven, the other group will go to hell. When the repentant die, angels come to escort them, but when the unrepentant die, evil spirits come to take them away. If you were to die, who do you think will come to escort you? Whom would you like to escort you? Of course, you would like the angels to come. Then I wish that you would at once rely upon the blood of Jesus, confess all your sins, and cut off all your sins.

Conclusion

In conclusion, the boisterous wind makes you doubt or disbelieve the prophecies or words of God concerning your life. Do you doubt God's words over that situation? Do you disbelieve that God cannot give you that joy you want? His grace is made available to us. Believe and have faith in Him and you shall succeed greatly.

Chapter 8

The Second Wind: The Wind of Holy Spirit

T he second wind also called the wind of the Holy Spirit is the wind of the gift of the Holy Spirit from God to His followers. Through this wind, there would be an exploration of the fresh fillings of the Holy Spirit. With the help of the Spirit, believers in Christ Jesus would have the chance to live a spirit-filled life:

> *"And were all filled with the Holy Ghost, and began to speak with tongues, as the Spirit gave them utterance" (Acts 2:4 KJV)*

> *"But the Comforter, which is the Holy Ghost, whom the Father will send in my name, he shall teach you all things, and bring all things to your remembrance..." (John 14:26 KJV)*

God's second wind or the wind of the Holy Spirit opens to us new and challenging ways. It refills our lives again with unspeakable joy and peace from God:

> *"Our mouths were filled with laughter, our tongues with songs of joy. Then it was said among the nations, "The Lord has done great things for them." The Lord has done great things for us, and we are filled with joy." (Psalm 126:2–3 NIV)*

The second wind of the Holy Spirit is a wind that changes indifferences, breaks fears, shatters doubts, creates a bold prayer life. It is the wind that will make us serve God better in a way that we never imagined or thought that we could:

> *"Therefore, my beloved brother, be steadfast, immovable, always abounding in the work of the*

> *Lord, knowing that in the Lord your labor is not in vain." (1 Corinthians 15:58 ESV)*

The second wind of the Holy Spirit frees us all as God's follower from suffering or hardship and releases us to live in the fullness of God's amazing grace:

> *"But after that the kindness and love of God our Saviour toward man appeared, not by works of righteousness which we have done, but according to his mercy he saved us, by the washing of regeneration, and renewing of the Holy Ghost..." (Titus 3:4–5 KJV)*

The wind also keeps us moving no matter what comes our way and what we face, and also through the wind, God forgives of us of our sins:

> *"If we confess our sins, he is faithful and just to forgive us our sins, and to cleanse us from all unrighteousness." (1 John 1:9 KJV)*

The wind also makes us soar higher with the Lord. It raises us up to standard level with God. It makes us do extraordinary things that we could never imagine we could do:

> *"But those who hope in the Lord will renew their strength. They will soar on wings like eagles; they will run and not grow weary, they will walk and not be faint." (Isaiah 40:31 NIV)*

The wind of the Holy Spirit is a wind that breaks every wall that is before us no matter how strong those walls may be:

> *"So the people shouted when the priests blew the trumpets. And it happened when the people heard the sound of the trumpet, and the people shouted with a great shout, that the wall fell down flat. Then the*

people went up into the city, every man straight before him, and they took the city." (Joshua 6:20 KJV)

The wind also gives unto mankind the wisdom to discern, proclaim, protect, name, and correct. Everything seen in the world today was wisdom made. Our reigning is tied to wisdom, and the wealth of this world is wisdom made:

"O Lord, how manifold are thy works! in wisdom hast thou made them all: the earth is full of thy riches." (Psalm 104:24 KJV)

"For who hath known the mind of the Lord, that he may instruct him? But we have the mind of Christ." (1 Corinthians 2:16 KJV)

The word "spirit" means breath or wind, so the Holy Spirit could literally be called the wind or breath of God *(John 20:22)*. Jesus compared the working of the Spirit to the moving of the wind. One of the symbols of the Holy Spirit in the Scripture is the wind, "the Spirit of God moved upon the face of the waters" *(Genesis 1:2 KJV)*.

"By the word of the LORD were the heavens made; and all the host of them by the breath of his mouth." (Psalm 33:6 KJV)

"And let it be, when thou hearest the sound of a going in the tops of the mulberry trees, that then thou shalt bestir thyself: for then shall the LORD go out before thee, to smite the host of the Philistines." (2 Samuel 5:24 KJV)

"And suddenly there came a sound from heaven as of a rushing mighty wind, and it filled all the house where they were sitting." (Acts 2:2 KJV)

The wind of the Holy Spirit is constantly blowing and we need the continual infilling, indwelling presence of the Holy Spirit. The wind serves as the most powerful force on the face of the earth and this confirmed that the Holy Spirit working in a believer is not by accident. Taking a look at the wind in nature, we can see what God can do in us and through us by His Spirit. This reveals God's doing in us and what seems impossible when our life is moved upon by the wind of the Holy Spirit.

The Wind Is a Transforming Force

The wind plays an important role in the transformation of the landscape. The constant blowing of the wind which helps in picking up dirt, sand, rock, and even trash over time will transform the appearance of the land. This is called "wind erosion." We are still a long way from where God wants us to be spiritually. God is constantly working on us, transforming us, and changing us to become what He wants us to be and be formed in us (Galatians 4:19).

> *"Till we all come in the unity of the faith, and of the knowledge of the Son of God, unto a perfect man, unto the measure of the stature of the fullness of Christ" (Ephesians 4:13 KJV)*

The "wind of Holy Spirit" blows in our lives to pick up the dirt, debris, and trash and burn it out. We need to allow the Holy Spirit wind to blow in our lives and rearrange things to suit Him because the wind bloweth where it desires. Some individuals resist God to work and move in their life, they never wanted God to rearrange things, shape them, form them, and mold them. They want to receive salvation and then leave things to suit themselves. To become what God desires us to be, we must allow "The wind blow where it wills" and blow out of our life what He wills.

The Wind Is a Power Generating Force

Since ages past, the wind has been used in sailing to carry ships and boats across the seas. This "wind of God" blowing in our life empowers us in our Christian walk and service.

> *"Not by might, nor by power, but by my spirit, saith the LORD of hosts." (Zechariah 4:6 KJV)*

> *"Whereunto I also labour, striving according to his working, which worketh in me mightily." (Colossians 1:29 KJV)*

Jesus commanded His disciples to "Go into all the world, preach the gospel, make disciples, but they must first 'Be filled with the Holy Ghost,'" and "Wait till you be endued with power from on high," He sent the Holy Spirit to empower us for service.

> *"The wind blows where it wishes, and you hear the sound of it, but cannot tell where it comes from and where it goes. So is everyone who is born of the Spirit." (John 3:8 NKJV)*

The Bible revealed that the Holy Spirit comes upon the sons of men, and makes them new creatures. Until we have an encounter with the Holy Spirit, we are "dead in trespasses and sins." We cannot discern the things of God because divine truths are spiritual and spiritually discerned, and unrenewed men are carnal and do not possess the power to search out the deep things of God.

In What Sense the Holy Ghost Is also Compared to the Wind?

The Holy Spirit, in His character compared Himself to dew, fire, oil, water in which our Savior uses the metaphor of wind. Jesus at once directed His attention to the wind, which is nonetheless real and operative because of its mysterious origin and operation. We cannot know where the wind comes from—it blows from the north or from the west. The spirit man discerns Him, feels Him, hears Him, and delights in Him, but neither with nor learning can lead a man into the secret. A believer may be bowed down with the weight of the Spirit's glory, or lifted up upon the wings of His majesty, but may not have an idea of how these feelings are caused in him. The fire of Holy Spirit at times gently fanned with the soft breath of divine comfort, or the deep sea of spiritual existence stirred with the mighty power of the Spirit's rebuke, but it is always a mystery how the eternal God comes in contact with the finite mind of His man creature, filling all heaven and yet dwelling in a human body as His temple. We all have believed in the Holy Spirit and therefore see Him, but if our faith needs sight to sustain it, we might never believe Him at all.

The real operations of the Spirit are due to God and to His sovereign will. Evangelists may stir up excitement with the best motives, and peoples' hearts warm until they begin to cry out, but all this will end in nothing unless it is divinely arranged. The wind does not only differ in force, but it differs in direction; the wind is always shifting. Perhaps there has never been two winds that blew exactly in the same direction. The wind blows as God directs, the Spirit of God does not always work with us—He does as He pleases; He comes and He goes. We can be in a happy hallowed mood at one time, and at another, we may have to cry, "Come from the four winds, oh breath!"

The Parallel between the Holy Ghost and the Effects of the Wind

The wind at times wails as if we could hear the cry far out at sea, or the meanings of the widows who must weep for them, the Spirit of God sets men wailing with an exceedingly bitter cry for sin, as one who is in sorrow for his firstborn, and at another time, the wind with a triumphant sound. So the Holy Spirit sometimes gives us faith, makes us bold, full of assurance, confidence, joy, and peace in believing. The Spirit of God comes into the soul sometimes and makes great contention with the work of the flesh. The wind reacts more than making a sound and this applies to the Holy Spirit. It works and produces results that are glaring and obvious.

The Holy Spirit is not to be feared as it is a blessed thing to rock and have our hopes tested and have carnal confidences shaken. So the Spirit of God comes and cleanses our evil thoughts and vain imaginations and brings spiritual healing to our soul. "There is not any peace, says my God, for the wicked." The wind is also helpful to those who avail themselves of such opportunity, God's Spirit is a mighty helper to those who will avail themselves of His influences. He assists that you see the flood gradually descending and your heart once more purified. We have found our utter inability to understand some part of divine truth. When the Spirit comes to the soul that is ready to receive influence, then He helps you to work in grace and bear up through all trials until you come to the place of peace and safety. Without the Spirit of God, we cannot do anything, and without our submission, He cannot work. We are to preach the gospel to every creature, and while one plants and another waters, God adds the increase. There is also a connection with the wind and human effort. It is a good and blessed thing to wait on God, watching for His hand and contentment, leaving all to Him.

In the testament, the word for *"spirit"* is *"ruach."* The Hebrew word *"ruach"* will mean **"spirit,"** **"wind,"** or perhaps *"breath."* In the New Testament, the word for *"spirit"* is *"pneuma,"* which can also mean *"wind"* or *"breath."* Of course, as far as the words and languages, there is much more to it than that, but for the sake of simplicity, just note that *"ruach"* and *"pneuma"* can mean *"spirit,"* *"wind,"* or *"breath."* Wind is a biblical symbol of the Holy Spirit.

> *"On the day of Pentecost, all the believers were meeting together in one place. Suddenly, there was a sound from heaven like the roaring of a mighty windstorm, and it filled the house where they were sitting." (Acts 2:1–2 NLT)*

Like the wind, the Holy Spirit comes in suddenly and from apparent obscurity—He whirls regarding the atmosphere and changes everything.

The Spirit, like the wind, moves wherever He wants and is at times unpredictable.

> *"Just as you can hear the wind but can't tell where it comes from or where it is going, so you can't explain how people are born of the Spirit." (John 3:8 NLT)*

Breath is additionally a biblical image of the Holy Spirit. The Holy Spirit is that the breath of God; He's the breath of life that sustains all living beings.

> *"And the Lord God formed man of the dust of the ground, and breathed into his nostrils the breath of life; and man became a living soul." (Genesis 2:7 KJV)*

> *"The spirit of God hath made me, and the breath of the Almighty hath given me life." (Job 33:4 KJV)*

The Holy Spirit yields from the depths of God. This is why when imparting the Holy Spirit to His followers, Jesus breathed upon them.

> *"Then He breathed on them and said, 'Receive the Holy Spirit.'" (John 20:22 NLT)*

The Holy Spirit is unpredictable, invisible but powerful. He brings refreshment, He stirs the atmosphere, and He brings life. He is the wind of heaven, the breath of God. The wind blows, we feel it, we sense it, but from where it comes, we don't exactly know. The wind of the Holy Spirit pours from heaven and brings one fantastic change within. In the Scripture, a comparison is made between the powerful operations of the Holy Spirit's wind and the blowing of earth's wind. *"The wind bloweth where it listeth, and thou hearest the sound thereof, but canst not tell whence it cometh, and whither it goeth: so is every one that is born of the Spirit" (John 3:8 KJV).* The wind of the Spirit, of course, has a different feel and a different work from earth's wind. Just as man cannot restrain the ability of the wind, neither can he restrain the power of God. We have no authority over either one. Although we cannot see the wind, we see its changing effects on the earth; we cannot see the Holy Spirit, but we see the changing effects He has in the lives of people who yield to Him. What a difference in the wind of the Holy Spirit brings about! We can't really comprehend it all, there are no words to adequately explain it, but we know it's a life-changing wind.

God Gave David This Message

"And it shall be, when thou shalt hear a sound of going in the tops of the mulberry trees, that then thou shalt go out to battle: for God is gone forth before thee to smite the host of the **Philistines**" *(1 Chronicles 14:15 KJV)*. The going in the tops of the mulberry trees, the wind of the Spirit, was David's sign. Like a howling, mighty wind, the Holy Spirit began to blow. David knew it was time to move, and the Lord delivered the Philistines into his hands. Take note of the actual fact that David waited for the wind of the Spirit, and then he went to claim the promised victory. Be careful to wait on the Lord.

A Mighty, Rushing Wind

In this Holy Ghost dispensation, the Holy Ghost blows the love of God and the humility of Jesus upon us daily. The wind of the Holy Spirit is blowing today with the same power it had on the Day of Pentecost. The Bible tells us in *Acts 2:2 KJV*, "And suddenly there came a sound from heaven as of a rushing mighty wind, and it filled all the house where they were sitting." The glory of the Lord was there, great action. With forked tongues of fireplace, this mighty wind blew upon those devoted saints who were waiting in the Upper Room for the promise of the Father. It crammed the entire house with the wind of the Spirit. Tabernacles of clay were baptized with the good

Holy Ghost then, and tabernacles of clay are baptized with the good Holy Ghost today.

The wind of the Spirit blows the good love of God into your heart; there is not any lack of God's love. After the cold, cold winter, you rejoice in the warmth of a gentle spring breeze. The wind of the Holy Spirit feels even higher for it's a lot larger. It warms your spirit and helps you yield to the Lord, makes you more conscious of Him.

Signs, Wonders, Miracles, and Healings

The love of God is shed abroad in our hearts by the Holy Spirit that is given unto North American nation *(Romans 5: 5).* For the Holy Ghost to shed the love of God in our hearts is wonderful indeed. The blowing of the Spirit is the signal to every true believer that Jesus is soon coming; it gives us strength and vision to take Jesus to the whole world in this final hour. We will not fail. All nations must hear this marvelous plan of salvation; a message confirmed with signs, wonders, miracles, and healings—and then the end will come. As the wind of the Spirit blows upon the nations, we tend to see the results. Miracles bring people to God. We have had over one hundred thousand people saved in one service; the evangelism spirit, the blowing of the Holy Spirit was upon the people, revealing Calvary to them, delivering them as the love of God poured upon them. When God's love wind blows upon individuals within the crusades, we see them change; the wind of the Spirit rushes in and the devils flee before that mighty power. In one overseas crusade service, almost 30,000 received the Holy Spirit. The Lord prophesied that it was just the beginning. Then in service in Uganda, we saw 64,574 numbered by God and baptized in the Holy Spirit. I was almost in heaven that evening! The crowd was estimated to be over 200,000. Never has it been known in the history of man that so many people received the baptism of the Holy Ghost in one service. Thousands of miracles and healings befell because of the wind of the Spirit's unbroken processing. What love, what greatness!

We have the record of only a few of the miracles Jesus performed when He was on earth. John wrote: "There are also many other things which Jesus did…if they should be written, the world could not contain them" (John 21:25 paraphrased). How wonderful it would be to know them all. Jesus, through the facility of the Holy Ghost, is still offering miracles today as the wind of the Spirit blows across the land.

The Power of the Resurrection

When the wind came on the Day of Pentecost, it brought every bit of power that the Lord spoke of. All the love of Calvary, all the love that went into Christ's death on the cross, was in that wind; the knowledge and power of His resurrection. Paul wasn't in the Upper Room with the rest of the apostles; at that time, he was still persecuting believers. But after his conversion, we read these thrilling words: "That I may know him, and the power of his resurrection, and the fellowship of his sufferings, being made conformable unto his death *(Philippians 3:10 KJV)*. Those in the Upper Room weren't praying that they might know the power of His resurrection; they knew it. It was in the wind. When they came down from the Upper Room, they staggered, fell under the power of the Holy Ghost until the people outside thought they were drunken. The prophecy of Joel came breezing through the wind of the Spirit and fell on Peter, and he began to quote prophecy. Typically, that was spoken by the prophet Joel, "And it shall come to pass in the last days, saith God, I will pour out of my Spirit upon all flesh" *(Acts 2:16–17 KJV)*.

The apostles were put in jail, but that didn't stop them. The more they were persecuted, the more they told the story of Jesus. Stephen, the first martyr, gloried in the wind of the Spirit as he told his accusers about Jesus. "When they heard these things, they were cut to the heart, and they gnashed on him with their teeth. But he, being filled with the Holy Ghost, looked up steadfastly into heaven, and saw the glory of God, and Jesus standing on the right hand of God, and said, Behold, I see the heavens opened, and the Son of man standing on the right hand of God" *(Acts 7:54–56 KJV)*. Stephen's forgiving spirit praised the

Lord as the stones pounded down on him. When the wind of the Spirit is processing, you have no trouble loving everyone. Keep that wind of affection and style moving upon you daily; the wind full of the grace of God, the strength of the Almighty. Be conscious when the Holy Spirit is moving for you and upon you, conscious of the wind of the Holy Spirit.

You can hear earth's wind at completely different times—from when it blows until exhausting once it dies down. You feel that wind, use it in different ways and at different times. You don't know the total strength of it, and so is it with the wind of the Holy Spirit. Its strength is beyond understanding, but you use it. People use the wind on earth to come up with power, and therefore, the wind of the Spirit furnishes power for America, power from on high to try and do the work God has planned. Some people have never felt the Spirit even though they have been going to church for years. If you have never experienced the wind of the Spirit, it's time to seek Him with your whole heart.

The Fruit and Gifts of the Spirit

The wind of the Spirit, remember, is a sign to every true child of God that Jesus is soon coming—it's in the wind of the Spirit. All the power of God that you could ever need and more, you will find in the wind of the Spirit. The nine gifts and nine fruits of the Spirit are there. In the Acts of the Apostles, we don't read of the Church seeking either the fruit or the gifts of the Spirit; they didn't need to, they had them. In the Acts of the Apostles, we see glorious results of the wind of the Holy Spirit, the gracious love, the miraculous changes in lives. Peter preaching to the crowed many of whom had cried for Jesus's death, he stood before them fearlessly, told them they had crucified Jesus. He had been within the wind of the Spirit and not was afraid to measure or die for the sake of his Master. If you have ever been in the wind of the Spirit, you surely have seen the hand of Jesus moving for you and the grace of God abounding. In the wind of the Spirit, you felt His faith coming upon you. What strength, what power it brought!

The early church depended on that strength and power. In fasting and prayers, they kept the wind blowing. It didn't blow once in a while; it moved mightily every day, and the fruits and gifts of the Spirit were in operation. That's the way it will be upon the Bride, saith the Lord, in this final hour. The winds of the Spirit are going to be processing upon her together with his love, grace, power. As the fruits of the Spirit become dominant among the bridal company, it will be unthinkable to them to do anything other than the whole will of God. But the fruit of the Spirit is love, joy, peace, longsuffering, gentleness, goodness, faith, meekness, temperance—against such there is no law. And those who are Christ's have crucified the flesh with the affections and lusts *(Galatians 5:22–24).* The gifts of the Spirit are listed in *1 Corinthians 12:7–11 KJV: "But the manifestation of the Spirit is given to every man to profit withal. For to one is given by the Spirit the word of wisdom; to another the word of knowledge by the same Spirit; to another faith by the same Spirit; to another the gifts of healing by the same Spirit; to another the working of miracles; to another prophecy; to another discerning of spirits; to another diverse kinds of tongues; to another the interpretation of tongues: But all these worketh that one and the selfsame Spirit, dividing to every man severally as he will."*

I say once more, all the fruits and gifts were in the wind of the Spirit, blowing on the early church.

The early church dined with the Spirit, went with Him, were encouraged and embraced by Him with all the greatness of Jesus Christ. Living in the wind of the Holy Spirit, they talked like Jesus, won souls and were about their Father's business just like He was. Bringing within the harvest, they centered their thoughts, their song, on Jesus, Jesus, Jesus. It was a blessed, wonderful time in the Spirit. The wind of the Spirit caressed the church as individuals yielded to it and the devil didn't have an opportunity. During the first thirty-three years, neither devil nor man could stop the church of Jesus Christ. The church was alive. The wind of His love and charm, the wind of His hope and faith, the wind of His compassion for lost souls blew upon the church and made God's greatness a living reality to its members. But things were about to change.

Winds Began to Blow

The day came when not as many people were being saved; not as many baptized in the Holy Ghost as in the very beginning. Darkness closed in more and more. As time went on, the wind of the Spirit almost ceased to blow. Loving the sick winds of the flesh of the devil, people responded to them instead of the wind of the Holy Spirit. They forgot the Upper Room experience; they even forgot Calvary and invented their own paths to glory like the inhabitants of Babel who had tried to build a tower all the way to heaven. Works of the flesh took over the church of Jesus Christ. The winds brought in lukewarmness, indifference, and disobedience to contaminate their once holy fellowship. What a wretched day that was once the unwell winds of the devil began processing into the house of God!

The sick winds of the devil are listed in *Galatians 5*. Paul, reproving the church wrote, "Ye did run well; who did hinder you that ye should not obey the truth? This persuasion cometh not of him that calleth you. A little leaven leaveneth the whole lump" *(Galatians 5:7–9 KJV)*. "Now the works of the flesh are manifest, which are these; Adultery, fornication, uncleanness, lasciviousness, idolatry, witchcraft, hatred, variance, emulations, wrath, strife, seditions, heresies, envyings, murders, drunkenness, revellings, and such like: of the which I tell you before, as I have also told you in time past, that they which do such things shall not inherit the kingdom of God" (Galatians 5:19–21 KJV). Today in the church, as a whole, much false doctrine is found. Those sick winds that brought the works of the flesh into the first church and ruined it are still being manifested nowadays.

Speak as the Spirit Gives Utterance

In the wind of the Spirit, people speak in tongues only as the Spirit gives utterance. And they were all stuffed with the Holy Spirit and started to talk with alternative tongues as the Spirit gave them utterance *(Acts 2:4)*. Not by their own will did they speak in tongues. Why should they when the Holy Spirit is a person alive within? The

Holy Spirit uses a person's vocal organs. He speaks through the person as He takes over the tongue. People are not to talk for the Holy Spirit; He speaks for Himself. The reason those who speak in tongues haven't any wind of the Spirit processing upon them is that they need to grieve the Spirit. They tried to speak in tongues themselves and didn't let the Holy Ghost speak. Not only that they try to teach others to speak at will instead of letting the Holy Ghost speak. No surprise, they don't live holy. They're not living within the wind of the Holy Spirit. If they were, they would know better than to try to talk for the Holy Ghost.

Those waiting in the Upper Room did not speak for the Holy Spirit. He Himself spoke through them. No one taught anyone else to speak in tongues in the Upper Room; it was all done by the Holy Ghost. No one was told to start talking baby talk, as some are told today, in an effort to speak in tongues at will. Sincere people will run from such false doctrine. The wind of spiritual truth is processing currently upon the children of God, separating the dedicated and consecrated from those who are not, those who, among other things, talk in tongues at will. The Lord told me that speaking in tongues at will is not of Him, that it grieves His Spirit. In some cases, flesh is doing the speaking; in other cases, it is the devil: a foreign spirit has entered and is talking. The Spirit of God is aggrieved, and His working is hindered. The Lord will not allow false doctrine in His church to continue indefinitely; He is separating and bringing together people who will accept all the Lord has said, accept the reality of the Holy Spirit, and seek the true baptism in the Holy Ghost as the early church had in the beginning. The idea of speaking in tongues or praying in tongues at will is absurd to the Bride. When the Holy Spirit prays through me, I have nothing to do with it. I pray in English until He takes over, and then He does the praying, not I. That's the reason He thrills me so much.

Jesus said, "No man will return to *me*, except the Father which hath sent me draw him: and I will raise him up at the last day" *(John 6:44)*. No man can come to God unless he is drawn by the Spirit. Any congregation of people that do not have the perfect love of Jesus is missing the wind of the Holy Spirit. That excellent wind brings the right love, grace, forgiveness, humility of God. The perfect wind brings the perfect holiness of God, the perfect righteousness, goodness and faith, the perfect everything. Thank God for the wind of the Holy Spirit!

Elijah Ran in the Power of the Spirit

First *Kings 18:4–46*, And it came to pass in the meanwhile, that the heaven was black with clouds and wind, and there was a great rain. And Ahab rode and went to Jezreel. And the hand of the LORD was on Elijah, and he girded up his loins and ran before Ahab to the entrance of Jezreel. It had not rained for three-and-a-half years, and Elijah on Mt. Carmel sent his servant seven totally different times to ascertain for a symbol of rain. Finally, the seventh time, the servant saw a cloud the size of a man's hand. Who let him see that cloud? Who put it there? The Holy Spirit. Then the Holy Spirit took over Elijah, giving him supernatural power to outrun King Ahab's chariot. Think of the fine horses dashing before that chariot, yet Elijah outran them. It wasn't a standard violent storm that day; the wind of the Spirit was processing, unlocking the heavens that it had kept closed for three-and-a-half years. The earth's wind alone processing on Elijah couldn't have given him the facility to run before king, but the wind of the Spirit could. If this were a standard run, the Lord wouldn't have put it in the Bible; however, it was a miraculous flight. Elijah was exuberant, running in the Spirit, caught up in the glory of the wind.

With the help of the wind of the Holy Spirit in this last and final hour, it's time to run. "Thrill at the voice of my beloved! Behold, he cometh jumping upon the mountains, skipping upon the hills" (Song of Solomon 2:8). Let Logos carry you from mountain to mountain, skip with you upon the hills.

The Israelites Crossed by Faith

In this wind of the Spirit, constant greatness that separated the waters of the Red Sea numerous times a few years past is found. "And

Moses stretched out his hand over the sea; and the LORD caused the sea to go back by a strong east wind all that night, and made the sea dry land, and the waters were divided. And the children of Israel went into the midst of the sea upon the dry ground: and the waters were a wall unto them on their right, and on their left" *(Exodus 14:21–22 KJV)*. It was no normal wind that blew all night on the sea; it had been a wind with the facility to separate the waters, hold them back, and create a land road all through the Red Sea. Then the wind of the Spirit with all the facility of heaven let the waters go on pharaoh's army. Like iron, that army sank and was drowned. By faith, the Israelites crossed, and by sight, Pharaoh's army tried to do the same thing; but they didn't know the meaning of the wind of the Spirit, and were unable to do what God's people had done. Trying to do by sight what others are doing by faith simply will not work. Using sight instead of religion has caused several persons to doubt God.

Like the pharaoh, some see God moving for faithful people and think they will have the same results. When it doesn't happen, they blame God. They take note of the faithful people walking in the love and greatness of God and wonder why that greatness is not in their lives. The waters close in on them, and down they go. They are at fault for they don't use God's faith. They need to learn about the Holy Spirit. More and more people are learning about Him and going beyond their own human spirits into the Spirit of God. In the wind of the Spirit, ears are opened to what the Spirit is communicating. There is no room for doubt and fear in the warmth of the Spirit, no room for oppression and depression. The wind of the Spirit is blowing more and more into the house of God where true believers are shouting the wonderful praises of God and being separated unto the Lord. Drawing people with His mighty power, the Holy Spirit is separating them through the blood that stained the Old Rugged Cross, separating the very dedicated, the very consecrated, unto Himself.

Without Spot or Wrinkle

Leading the Bride by a mighty hand, the Holy Spirit is shouting again and again that no spot can be found in this one…or this one…or this one. The blessed Groom, Jesus, is looking upon the Bride saying, "Thou art all fair, my love; there is no spot in thee" *(Song of Solomon 4:7)*. When prophet will whisper that to the Bride, no power will be able to stop her. The Bride is a mighty force as she goes into battle against the devil, for the greatness of God goes with her. Going forth to usher in the loss despite the price, in love with Jesus and not with herself, the Bride yields completely to Him. The wind of the Holy Spirit is flowing with all of heaven's favor upon her at all times. The fierce anger of God against the works of the devil is manifested in the wind of the Spirit. Unafraid, the Bride tramples devils underfoot. Clothed in the wind of the Spirit through the mighty blood of Jesus of Nazareth, she will not be denied as she shouts the praises of the Lord. The strength and power of the wind of the Holy Spirit will bring victory. Thank God for the wind of Spirit! Thank God that the Holy Spirit is blowing upon earth today! As the Holy Ghost reveals Himself, a great mystery of God is indeed becoming clear.

Children of God initially perceive the good mystery of salvation, that it's real. Then the great mystery of the Holy Ghost coming in to live and dwell on the inside takes us into the deeper reality of the Lord. Remember, He sets up His abode in tabernacles of clay today just as He set up His abode in tabernacles of clay on the Day of Pentecost. In our spirits we hear the sound of the abundance of the rain of the Holy Spirit; listen to the great sound of it and rejoice. It will blow harder and harder to wake everyone who can be awakened, to bring everyone possible into the reality of Jesus.

Jesus Is the Bride's Song

Jesus is the Bride's love song, her joy all day long: Jesus, Jesus, Jesus! She will speak the name Israelite with all the love of heaven. Devils will tremble before her. She will speak the name Jesus and the earth will shake with the greatness of God. She will speak the name Jesus and the blind will receive sight, the crippled will be made whole, and the dumb will speak. People will be delivered from all manner of sicknesses and diseases and the devil-possessed set free from all the terrible demonic powers that had possessed them. Jesus said, "And these signs shall follow them that believe; In my name shall they cast out devils…they shall lay hands on the sick, and they shall recover" *(Mark 16:17–18 KJV).* Jesus believers will cast out devils. Why should we be afraid of demons when we have been given power over them? Why should we back away afraid? Why shouldn't we be bold enough to speak the name Jesus? The wind of the Holy Spirit is blowing upon us.

If you keep within the wind of the Spirit, you can be within the divine will of God, day after day, night after night. This wind of the Spirit brings the perfect everything: the perfect gospel, the perfect love, the perfect faith, the perfect vision of this end-time hour, the perfect knowledge that Jesus is soon coming.

"Let not your heart be troubled: ye believe God, believe also in me" (John 14:1 KJV). The wind of the Spirit brings the knowledge of the perfect heaven we are going to. "In my Father's house are many mansions: if it were not so, I would have told you. I go to prepare a place for you. And if I go and prepare a place for you, I will come again, and receive you unto myself; that wherever I am, there ye may be also" *(John 14:2–3 KJV).* Jesus will come again. In the wind of the Holy Spirit, you discover His message: "I will be able to come! I soon will come!"

Praise the Lord All Ye People!

The cry of the Spirit is for this harvest time. The harvest is ripe, oh Bride of Christ; bring it on in! You have the help, the strength you need. Angels have joined you for the harvest. If you need ten thousand or ten million angels to help, you will be supplied. Oh, Bride, nothing you need will be withheld from you. The host of heaven will back you up as you work for the Master in these harvest fields. Blessed be the name of the Lord! In the wind of the Spirit, praise time is all the time. Continually praising God, you go forth for Him. Paul lived in the wind of the Holy Spirit, and he told people to always praise God: "Praise the Lord, all ye Gentiles; and laud him, all ye people" (Romans 15:11). In prison, out of prison, in the valleys, and on the mountaintops, Paul praised God. The wind of the Holy Spirit was blowing on Paul wherever he was.

The wind of the Spirit is found in the greatness of Calvary, the Resurrection, and the Ascension. The Spirit of truth has come. Jesus said, "And ye shall know the truth, and the truth shall make you free" (John 8:32). The wind of the Spirit holds nothing but the truth—the wind of the Spirit is the Spirit of truth. *"Even the Spirit of truth; whom the planet cannot receive, because it seeth him not, neither knoweth him: but ye know him; for he dwelleth with you, and shall be in you" (John 14:17 KJV).* "But once the Comforter has return, whom I will send unto you from the Father, even the Spirit of truth, which proceedeth from the Father, he shall testify of me" *(John 15:26 paraphrased).* "Howbeit when he, the Spirit of truth, is come, he will guide you into all truth: for he shall not speak of himself; but whatsoever he shall hear, that shall he speak: and he can show you things to come back *(John 16:13 KJV).* No false doctrine is found in the Spirit of truth. Those who live in the wind of the Spirit are free, for the truth, Jesus, has set them free. Are you really free today? Are you living in the wind of the truth? The wind of the Holy Spirit?

Called-Out People

The Bride can take up wherever the Book of Acts stops. She will not fall victim to the stumbling blocks that caused the early church to drift away from the whole truth of God. The Bride will go forth with the wind of the Spirit, the greatness of the Almighty as the favor of God rests upon her. The Holy Spirit is an actual person. He lives and dwells within tabernacles of clay that are cleansed by the blood of Jesus, rejoicing, blessing, singing, preaching, and testifying. Sanctifying blood power within the wind of the Spirit cleanses the soul of all sin. When the soul is ready, the tongue sanctified, the Holy Ghost moves in. For Him to continue to stay, the person must keep the tongue clean. Don't be deceived into thinking you can do whatever you want and still have the Holy Ghost. He won't stay where there is uncleanness.

While the unwell winds are processing, influencing many, there still is a called-out person, separated from a separated people: the Bride of Christ. She is perfect in His love, perfect in obedience toward Him. She has His greatness, His goodness to serve others with hands so like the serving hands of Jesus. Her willing heart rejoices in doing anything for Him. The tears of Calvary are in her life—not salty tears, but the tears of grace and love, the tears of His mercy, compassion, and yearning. Oh, how she is crying! And the Holy Spirit is crying with her. In this great hour of the pouring out of the Holy Spirit, we don't fear the ill winds when we are separated into the truth, pure truth of God. "Jesus said unto him, I am the way, the truth, and the life: no man cometh unto the Father, but by me *(John 14:6 KJV)*. Know the truth; know Jesus. No false philosophical system is at intervals with the Bride, and that which is without doesn't tear down that which is within. We needn't tremble because of the things coming on the earth; our hearts are steadfast, unmovable, rooted, and grounded in the truth, Jesus Christ. As we walk in the footsteps of the holiness of His grace, the holiness of His life, every stride takes us closer and closer to Rapture ground. One day, the wind of the Spirit can catch the Bride away. Without the wind of the Spirit, you won't go; without the Holy Ghost, you won't be taken in the Rapture. To be changed you will need the baptism of the Holy Ghost.

"Behold, I show you a mystery; we tend to shall not all sleep, however, we tend to shall all be modified, in a moment, within the twinkling of an eye, at the last trump: for the trumpet shall sound, and also the dead shall be raised incorrupt, and that we shall be modified *(1 Corinthians 15:51–52 paraphrased)*. Jesus will come again, and the wind of the Spirit is blowing mightily to catch the Bride away on wings of love and greatness. The winds of the Spirit are mounting higher and higher, and soon we will be at the gate of glory! It won't take long—a twinkling of an eye—for this supernatural wind, this supernatural power to lift us to heaven.

"And he rode upon a cherub, and did fly: and he was seen upon the wings of the wind." (2 Samuel 22:11 KJV)

The Lord was seen on the wings of the wind of the Spirit, the wings of love and greatness. The Bride, too, will ride on the wind of the Spirit. Man can't harness the winds of earth; he can't soar very high into the sky without protection, but in the wind of the Spirit, man can go all the way to heaven. It's a supernatural wind.

All the greatness of God is in the wind of the Holy Spirit. When the wind blew through the tops of the mulberry trees for David, it meant victory. As the wind blows for the Bride, it means additional and additional victories. In the mighty wind of God's love, the Lord is reaching out for the heathen with His grace, making the blood of Jesus become real to them.

Win the Lost at Any Cost

Are you crying out night and day for the lost? My heart yearns to reach them all, to tell them the story of Jesus. I live to bring to them the wind of the Holy Spirit. They have felt the ill winds of the devil; in some parts of the world, they have sacrificed their own children. It's a terrible thing, offering children to Satan! But, oh God, what a thrill to see parents hand their children over to the Lord—that's what the wind of the Spirit is bringing about today. The wind of the Spirit is blowing more and more upon the heathen, to give them hope that something good is about to happen for them, they don't know just what. We must reach them with the message of Jesus to let them know the wonder in the wind of the Holy Spirit. We must not fail in multitudes; multitudes without number will die and go to hell. God help us not to fail! Help us to live, walk, dine in the place the wind of the Spirit is blowing.

The wind of the Spirit won't blow where it is not welcomed. Many people have rejected it, blasphemed, and the wind of the Spirit will never blow upon them. There are people on planet Earth, saith the

Lord, on whom the wind of His Spirit will never blow again. The Lord blew His Spirit upon them, but they wanted no part of it. They have rejected Him. Some have mocked Him, some have declared the wind of His Spirit is of the devil, others have declared the ill winds of the devil are the Spirit of God. The devil is an arch deceiver. From one and all, the soul will take its departure, but even before that, a living, spiritual death has sealed the doom of many. How unhappy to grasp that some individuals alive and walking on earth nowadays are dead to God! By rejecting the Holy Spirit, they have brought spiritual death upon themselves. Never will they have another invitation or another chance to get right with God. When you are dead to God, you are doomed to hell for all eternity. No life at all exists outside of God. Just as the Lord one day will withdraw all His life from those who have blasphemed, He will draw His children from His life. No one will come back unto the Lord unless they're drawn by the Spirit. It's dangerous to mock God, to insult the Spirit of God. Classify God's power and the wind of the Spirit as the power, and the wind of the devil is blasphemy.

Jesus spoke of blaspheming the Spirit after He had delivered a devil-possessed person who was also blind and dumb. But once the Pharisees detected it, they said, "This fellow doth not cast out devils but by Beelzebub the prince of the devils. And Jesus knew their thoughts, and said unto them, Every kingdom divided against itself is brought to desolation, and every city or house divided against itself shall not stand: And if the Satan cast out Satan, he is divided against himself; how shall then his kingdom stand? And if I by Beelzebub cast out devils, by whom do your children cast them out? therefore they shall be your judges. But if I cast out devils by the Spirit of God, then the kingdom of God has come unto you *(Matthew 12:24–28 KJV)*. "Wherefore I say unto you, All manner of sin and blasphemy shall be forgiven unto men: but the blasphemy against the Holy Ghost shall not be forgiven unto men. And whosoever speaketh a word against the Son of man, it shall be forgiven him: but whosoever speaketh against the Holy Ghost, it shall not be forgiven him, either in this world, neither in the world to come" (Matthew 12:31–32 KJV). When Jesus said blasphemy against the Holy Ghost would never be forgiven in this world or in the world to come, He was speaking of the unforgivable sin. People who want a resurrection from their sins can have it through the wind of the Holy Spirit. The wind of the Spirit brings them into the realization that they need Jesus, that Calvary is the reality, that the blood of Jesus is all powerful, that there are a real devil and a real hell, and unless they repent, they are going there. Convicted of their sins, many will cry, "What must I do to be saved!" the Bride in the form of Peter will answer: "Repent, and be baptized every one of you in the name of Jesus Christ for the remission of sins, and ye shall receive the gift of the Holy Ghost" *(Acts 2:38 KJV).*

Be Ye Holy

The wind of the Spirit comes from one great source—Lord God Almighty. We don't know everywhere it goes; we don't understand how it can penetrate our innermost being, how it can go inside and change men, women, boys, and girls, making them new creations. We don't dare say we understand it all, we just know it happens. Thank the living God for His Spirit, for the power of His greatness, for the Old Rugged Cross; thank God for the truth! The truth gives us sight, lights our paths, and shows us the way of God. Truth makes the Holy Spirit and the many ways He works. We embrace the Lord's great manifestations; we delight in them. Eagerly, we reach out to get all of Him we possibly can so that we might serve all the greatness of Jesus Christ to the multitudes. The Holy Ghost is our teacher, our guide, our director. He is the one to help us serve Jesus to a lost and dying world. Do not fail or be disobedient, do not be unholy in any way, but be pure, clean like Jesus Himself. No guile can be allowed to be found in us. Peacemakers, we must be seasoned with love and grace so that our tongues may be used by the Holy Spirit to bless others. This is the nice pouring out time, and the true Church is coming out of the darkness and sins of the past. While many are saying that no one can live holy, the holy Church is coming forth, separated unto the Lord for this great final time of harvest. The people who are holy are the ones the Lord will use. "Because it is written, Be ye holy; for I am holy" *(1 Peter 1:16 KJV).*

Jesus said, "Follow thou me" *(John 21:22 KJV)*. The disciples could not keep with Jesus when He was here. It was not till once He went away that they might actually follow Him, not until the Holy Ghost came to set up His abode inside their hearts. The only way we will be able to keep up with the Master in this final hour is to be yielded to the wind of the Holy Spirit, the wind of love, grace, power, and greatness. Heaven's winds are blowing through the power of the Holy Ghost. Yea, saith the Spirit of the Lord: "I'm in the midst of this people, and I am here to do great things for you. I am here to open your eyes to all of my greatness. I am here to open your ears so you can hear what the Spirit is saying. I am here to open your understanding to my greatness and give you knowledge of how I will use my true people in this final hour. I will work and do unbelievable things. I will work through my true people, and I will perform miracles, miracles, miracles, miracles in abundance to show and manifest my love for the lost throughout the whole earth. The heathen will look and behold and see my mighty hand moving, and multitudes will be turned to righteousness. They will be brought into my truth because my people will live the truth, my people will dwell in the truth, and my people will have heaven's life through my truth and heaven's strength. I will use my individuals in perfection during this their final hour. Oh my people that are called by my name: never be troubled. As you investigate the enemy, know that I am your strength and I am your help, and I am your high tower. Follow me, and no defeat can come to you. Follow me, and I will use you to bring in my harvest. Follow me, and one day, heaven will be yours and multitudes, multitudes that you have brought into the kingdom. I am moving, and my mighty power and the wind of my Spirit is truly blowing upon my true people to bring health, physical health, and spiritual health to my people so that they can do my work in this the final hour," saith the Lord.

Benefits of the Second Wind (The Wind of the Holy Spirit)

1. Makes us have and enjoy the spiritual gift of the Holy Spirit.

    "But to each one is given the manifestation of the Spirit for the common good." (1 Corinthians 12:7 NASB)

2. Makes us soar higher in the races of life.
3. Gives unto us wisdom for discerning that which is good or bad.

    "As for you, the anointing you received from Him remains in you, and you do not need anyone to teach you. But as his anointing teaches you about all things and as that anointing is real, not counterfeit—just as it has taught you, remain in him." (1 John 2:27 NIV)

The Holy Spirit

The Holy Spirit is not some kind of cloud or some kind of smoke, He is not a light. He is a thing. The Holy Spirit is that the person of the Maker. The Holy Spirit is exactly like Jesus because He does not receive power because He is the power of God. The Holy Spirit is that the Spirit of truth. The Holy Spirit or the Holy Ghost is the third person of the Trinity. God manifests as God the Father, God the Son, and God the Holy Spirit. The Holy Spirit is referred to as "the Lord, the Giver of Life."

The Ministry of the Holy Spirit

After salvation, the greatest experience you could ever have in your life is the experience with the unseen person of the Holy Spirit. The existence of the Holy Spirit in our lives is for a particular purpose. The Holy Spirit in our lives carries out some special ministry, which will be examined bellow.

The Comforter

The Holy Spirit is our comforter. He is there to comfort us in time of pain and hardship. The Holy Spirit is the one who suffers with us. He bears all our sorrow as if it is own. He always with us.

The Counselor

When you receive the Holy Spirit, He automatically becomes your counselor. He is the one who gives you advice, a piece of legal advice. He instructs our inner man and gives unto us instructions through which our lives will be guided.

The Helper

The Holy Spirit is also our helper. When we receive Him into our life, He is there to help us out at every junction of our life. He does for us that which we want or that which we ask of.

The Intercessor

The Holy Spirit goes with us as our intercessor. Though He uses us to do the interceding process, He is our great intercessor. The only Spirit uses us to intercede for others is through our faith.

The Strengthener

The Holy Spirit is also our strengthener. He strengthens us and that is the reason why He is taking His own step to ensure that everything works out for us and also participate fully and actively in the process.

The Enlighten

The Holy Spirit is a friend we turn to for advice. He is watering us to refresh us. He is a comforter to cheer us. He is a teacher to teach us. He is a guide to lead us. He serves as the oil to make us shine and as a fire to cleanse us. He serves as a seal to make us safe. He is the witness for us to look up to. He is the power to help us pray. He is the fruit bearer and sap to make us grow. He is our reminder to help us remember God's promises.

The Manifestation of the Holy Spirit

The Holy Spirit manifests in certain areas of our lives in one way or another. His manifestation strengthens our hearts. We are filled with the Holy Spirit after accepting and confessing Jesus Christ as our personal Savior and Lord. On the Day of Pentecost, intercessors were filled with the Spirit and then experienced the manifestations of the Spirit, which included the sound of rushing wind, tongues of fire resting on all and spoke in a very language that they failed to understand. Those who observed them had various responses. Some were amazed and perplexed and others mocked the Spirit's work in them. We see identical responses to the activity of the Spirit these days. Some see the manifestations because the work of the Spirit is to get angry or confused. Many are skeptical, seeing manifestations only as fleshly behavior. We acknowledge that some animal mixture, imitation, or exaggeration does not invalidate the genuine work of the Spirit in others. Christians from each tradition have written of this manifestation through history, particularly in times of revival. Some fell beneath conviction of sin, while others experienced an inner work of healing of their heart or received an impartation for ministry.

Purposes of the Manifestations of the Holy Spirit

The fruit of manifestations

This is seen in the lives of believers. They have a large intimacy with God; impartations of affection, peace, joy, and the fear of God; freedom from bondage (fear, anger, bitterness, pain, lust, etc.); physical healings and emotional healing; empowering for ministry (healing the sick, prophesying, intercession, etc.); refreshment. This leads to and encourages more evangelism.

Enlarging of spiritual capacities

This involves the overcoming of inner bondages, tenderized emotions, empowering or ministering to others; impartations of love, peace, joy, sensitized to receive more prophetic impressions, the fear of the Lord, "pain killer" because the Spirit will a deep work on the center, etc. Manifestation as signs God generally uses a manifestation as an indication to others in order that we are going to listen to what the Spirit is oral communication. When the Spirit provides signs, we have a tendency to raise what that specific sign means that. How is that the Spirit victimization it to create up the Church? The signs purpose to our want for a deeper reference to the Spirit. Manifestations, healing, and other spiritual signs are like a billboard that declares that God is working. A manifestation may be a sign on condition that it signifies one thing that helps unfold the gospel and builds up the dominion or the lives of individuals.

The Holy Spirit is a light to enlighten us. He is a friend that we turn to for advice. He is water that refreshes our soul. He is a comforter that cheers us up. He is a teacher that teaches us all things that we need to know. He is the guide that leads us. He serves as oil to make us shine and as a fire to cleanse us. He is a dove that brings us mercy. He serves as a seal to make us safe. He is the witness that we look up to. He is the power to help us pray. He is the fruit bearer and sap to make us grow. He is our reminder to help us remember God's promises.

The Moves of the Holy Spirit: The Second Wind

In Christendom, there is an experience of New Birth. After a person has accepted Jesus Christ as his the personal Savior and has been baptized into the body of Christ as a member of God's family, there is another experience which awaits such individual that would bring him deeper into the things of God, deeper into the spiritual dimension. Such experience is the baptism of the Holy Spirit. A buoyant Spirit of joy and praises is a result of staying continually filled up with the Holy Spirit. Staying filled with the Holy Spirit does not only strengthen or renew us as a believer, but it produces the joyful spirit of praises, it also attracts the unbelievers and makes Him desire a similar experience. According to Paul, he said, that the believers need to be renewed or strengthened with might by God's spirit in their inner mind. The infilling of the Holy Spirit isn't sufficient justification for a particular day. There should be the daily renewal of our spirit in order for us to be strong spiritually. As believers, we need to stay filled with the Holy Spirit.

> *"And be not drunk with wine, wherein is excess, but be filled with the Spirit; speaking to yourselves in psalms and hymns and spiritual songs, singing and making melody in your heart to the Lord..."* *(Ephesian 5:18–19 KJV)*

The joy of our life is based on Jesus. Our joy is not based on those circumstances or that situation facing us presently or which surrounds our life but on Jesus Christ. We can continually maintain that buoyant spirit of joy and praises by focusing our attention on Him and also by allowing His spirit to renew our own spirit day by day. As we wait upon the Lord to renew our spirit, we have a role to play. During this period of waiting, we must seek God in His Word and in prayer.

> *"But they that wait upon the Lord shall renew their strength; they shall mount up with wings like eagles; they shall run, and not be weary; and they shall walk, and not faint."* *(Isaiah 40:31 KJV)*

The move of the Holy Spirit brings about different blessings and victories to our life. The move of the Spirit tells us or instructs us on what to do because through this, He will redeem our lives from destruction. With His move, we are going to be able to walk in joy, love, peace, longsuffering, gentleness, goodness, faith, meekness, and intemperance.

The moves of the Holy Spirit make us walk in the Spirit, so that He may keep us fully informed of the manners in which God would have us live. It makes us learn the ways of the Spirit so that we can trace God in all of the circumstances that form our daily life with Him. In thinking, God's thinking is not the same as ours.

"For as the heavens are higher than the earth, so are my ways higher than your ways, and my thoughts than your thoughts." (Isaiah 55:9 KJV)

When the Spirit moves, it leads you to do extraordinary things. After Jesus was born of the Spirit, the Spirit led Him into the wilderness to be tempted by the devils so that the name of God might be glorified. In life, whether we know it or not, there are things that would either make us or break us. In life, you will face one persecution or another. The devil will put up every tribulation he can, but when the Spirit moves, you get freed from them.

The move of the Spirit makes you come out with an opportunity to truly prove that God exists. Do you know that overcoming trials and temptation is an opportunity of faith for you to prove God exists? Some people during the time of trial and test get carried away with it because they have no faith that God really can see them through it. We need to learn the way the Spirit walks so that we, too, can walk that way. Let God have His way in your life. Stay put among the arduous place and you will eventually rest upon the mountain high.

The move of the Holy Spirit baptizes you into a deeper dimension of the Spirit. It makes us witness the good news of Christ to unbelievers. It gives unto us an undue power for the works of God. The moves of the Spirit make the wind of the Spirit sweep through our challenges in life.

The move of the Holy Spirit sustains us in the season of the hardship of life. It flows on us the rivers of living water. It gives us the heavenly birth in Christ Jesus.

"Jesus answered, 'Truly, truly I say to you, unless someone is born of water and the spirit, he is not able to enter into the kingdom of God. What is born of the flesh is flesh, and what is born of the Spirit is spirit. Do not be astonished that I said to you, "It is necessary for you to be born from above." The wind blows wherever it wishes, and you hear the sound of it, but you do not know where it comes from and

> ***where it is going. So is everyone who is born of the Spirit.'" (John 3:5–8 LEB)***

The move of the Holy Spirit also makes us enjoy or partake of the manifestation of the fruits of the Spirit. Through it, you have greater intimacy with God; the impartation of love, peace, joy, the fear of God, refreshing moment, physical healings, and emotional healing, empowering for ministry, freedom from bondage are the fruit of the Spirit that we enjoy. Holy Spirit moves to also enlarge our spiritual capacities. Give unto us the power to overcome bondage, tenderize emotions, to fear the Lord, and serve Him. It also makes the Spirit dwell in us for the discerning of our works.

> ***"Know ye not that ye are the temple of God, and that the Spirit of God dwelleth in you?" (1 Corinthians 3:16 KJV)***

God dwells in us individually and collectively. The body of each believer is a temple of God and the church, the whole body of believers is the temple of God also:

> ***"And what agreement hath the temple of God with idols? For ye are the temple of the living God..." (2 Corinthians 6:16 KJV)***

The move of the Holy Spirit (the second wind) can also empower and influence us by enabling us to do human abilities with divine enhancement when we have it in us. The move empowers us to be wise, powerful, and perform the salvation acts. In the Bible, there are some certain people whom the Spirit empowered. Joseph interpreted the pharaoh's dream that the pharaoh's magicians could not interpret. Bezalel, the son of Uri, was filled with the spirit of wisdom, understanding, and knowledge and all kinds of skills to make artistic designs.

> ***"And I have filled him with the spirit of God, in wisdom, and in understanding, and in knowledge, and***

in all manner of workmanship, to devise cunning works, to work in gold, and in silver, and in brass, and in cutting of stones, to set them, and in carving of timber, to work in all manner of workmanship."
(Exodus 31:3–5 KJV)

When the Spirit moves, it gives unto us the creative life. The Spirit enhances us to use our thoughts, abilities, and purpose to accomplish God's purposes; it enables us to do the will of that which created us (God), and also influences our mind to speak that which God wants to deliver to His people. The move of the Spirit also brings divine resurrection of life and death. The move also gives God gifts to His followers to empower us for the ministry work. The move of the Holy Spirit sets us apart for God's use. The moves explain to us spiritual truths. The moves pick apart America and restrain America from doing dangerous things.

"Nevertheless, I tell you that truth; it is expedient for you that I go away: for if I go not away, the Comforter will not come unto you; but if I depart, I will send him unto you. And when he is come, he will reprove the world of sin, and of righteousness, and of judgment: Of sin because they believe not on me; of righteousness, because I go to my Father, and ye see me no more..." (John 16:7–10 KJV)

Holy Spirit: Authorization of the Scriptures

The Holy Spirit possesses different names which help in producing the Scripture. These names are directly related to what the Bible teachers called "revelation" and "inspiration." Revelation is the uncovering, a bringing to light of that which had been previously wholly hidden or only obscurely seen. God has been pleased in different ways to make a supernatural revelation of Himself and His purposes and plan. Inspiration is the extraordinary or supernatural guidance of the writers of the Scripture by the Holy Spirit, whereby they wrote the divine Word of God. In both cases, the act of God was made known.

The authorization of the Scripture by the Holy Spirit will thus be examined in the following ways:

The spirit of revelation

One of the authorships names of the Holy Spirit is "the spirit of revelation." He is the spirit of revelation because He revealed the truth to the apostles and prophets as they, with Him, wrote the Scripture. The spirit, in one way or another, revealed to the apostles and the prophets what to do at a particular time or another.

The Spirit of the Holy God

In the Book of Daniel 4:8, King Nebuchadnezzar called the spirit who revealed the truth to David the "Spirit of the Holy God."

> *"But at the last Daniel came in before me, whose name was Belteshazzar, according to the name of my God, and in whom is the spirit of the holy gods: and before him, I told the dream, saying..." (Daniel 4:8 KJV)*

In this Bible verse, the spirit of God revealed unto Daniel the meaning of vision and dreams, which could not be either understood nor know through mean of divination or appeals to false gods. In Daniel, King Nebuchadnezzar was confident that he will interpret the dream because Daniel possesses interpretive abilities.

The spirit of the prophets

The Holy Spirit indwelling in the prophets allows them and gives them spirit to control. In writing the Scripture, the Spirit supernaturally guides each to write the Word of God accurately and without error. The Spirit allows the writing style of the author to shine through that Word. The Spirit impacts in those writers (prophets) the power to communicate the Word of God to His people.

The wind

A fourth authorship name of the Holy Spirit is the emblem of the Holy Spirit as "the wind." Peter used this word to picture a ship being moved along the waves by catching the wind in its sail. Just as the wind blows leaves or kite in a certain direction, the Holy Spirit also blows the human in a certain direction as they wrote His Scripture.

The spirit of truth

The title of the Holy Spirit emphasizes the intimacy and integrity of the Scripture. The spirit of truth is the good and perfect will of God. It makes the Scripture writer to write in truth and in the, Spirit which enables us Christians to study those words and be confident in it, and through it, we also shares it to those around us.

The spirit of prophecy

The spirit of prophecy stresses the role of the Holy of the Spirit beyond His guiding of the Scripture writers to ensure that the message itself was inspired. One of the abiding natures of the Holy Spirit is to glorify Christ; therefore, the testimony of Jesus is the spirit of prophecy.

> *"And I fell at his feet to worship him. And he said unto me, See thou do it not: I am thy fellowservant, and of thy brethren that have the testimony of Jesus: worship God: for the testimony of Jesus is the spirit of prophecy." (Revelation 19:10 KJV)*

The Holy Spirit: Our Creator

The Holy Spirit is our creator. He created us in His own image (male and female). He gave unto us the breath of life so that we might live and be in charge of the whole earth. The Holy Spirit proved His creative nature in the following ways:

The finger of God

This word was used by God to make us know how the Scripture describes the works of the Holy Spirit in another way. Just as an artist uses his or her hands or fingers in creating a painting or beautiful piece of pottery, so is the finger of God or the hand of God—a reference to the creative nature of the Holy Spirit that adds beauty, scope, and dimension to the world. The Holy Spirit is at work to make creation attractive, appealing, and pleasing to mankind. The Holy Spirit, as our creator, brings into existence matters, such as the gathering of physical land mass and the arrangement of the geography of this world.

The voice of the Lord

Various "voice names" of the Holy Spirit also imply His participation in the creation process. An appreciation of the creative work of the voice of the Lord is a foundation to a healthy and growing faith in God. By faith, we tend to perceive that the world was framed by the word of God in order for the items that are seen aren't fabricated from things that are visible. As a result of the creation exercise, His voice directs our life and guides us in our daily doings.

The breath of life

The Holy Spirit was portrayed as the breath, the breath of the Almighty, the breath of God, the breath of life, the breath of the Lord, and "the breath of Your nostrils." He was also portrayed as the spirit of land by other names emphasizing His life-giving and life-sustaining ability.

> *"And the LORD God formed man of the dust of the ground, and breathed into his nostrils the breath of life, and man became a living soul." (Genesis 2:7 KJV)*

The involvement of the Spirit in the creation resulted in the order, design, beauty, and the life of creation today.

The Ministry of the Holy Spirit: Our Spiritual Guide

The Holy Spirit, our guide, performs some works or ministry in our life as a believer. Some of this ministry will thus be examined below:

The spirit of access

The Holy Spirit gives balance to our life as a believer and provides entrance for us into the heavenly places. Through the Holy Spirit, we have access to the family of God in salvation and access to God by prayer. When we pray, we do so because of the ministry of "the Spirit of grace and supplication" in our lives. The Holy Spirit also gives unto us a new life when we are born again.

The spirit of indwelling

The Holy Spirit can be portrayed as the spirit of indwelling. As a Christian, we enjoy immediately the indwelling of the Holy Spirit when we give our lives to Christ. The biblical teaching concerning the indwelling of the Holy Spirit should motivate us to personal holiness. Through the Holy Spirit in teaching, we have the grace given to us to know how to live a holy life. The Christian life is the life of God living through us. Having the Holy Spirit indwelling every Christian makes it possible for every Christian to live a holy life.

The spirit of unity

The Holy Spirit makes unity among Christians possible by empowering each of us to live a Christian life and also by placing us into a single body—the body of Christ. In this way, the Holy Spirit has established the conditions by which unity can be enjoyed. When a sense of unity is absent in a group of Christians, the Holy Spirit is being hindered. In such cases, believers may be fighting God or simply refusing to allow the Holy Spirit to control their lives.

The spirit of fullness

The fullness of the Holy Spirit is important to the experience of living the normal Christian life. When the Holy Spirit fills our lives, the Holy Spirit gets more of us. We do more for the works of God; we yield ourselves more to the things of His kingdom. Christians are filled with the Holy Spirit as they confess their sins to God.

The spirit of fruitfulness

The Holy Spirit is also referred to or portrayed as the spirit of fruitfulness because it produces spiritual fruits in our lives. Just as a fruit on a tree is the result of growth within the tree, the same is the fruit in the Christian life, which is the result of the Holy Spirit working in and through us for the perfection of the works of the Spirit.

How to Receive the Blessing of the Holy Spirit

Firstly, we must, through the power of the Spirit, realize the scene in which we are to labor. In this case, the Holy Spirit took the prophet Ezekiel and carried him out and set him down in the midst of the valley which was full of dry bones. This is just a type of what will happen to every man whom the Spirit means to use and bless. Do you want to save people in the slums? Do you want to bring back that lost sheep? Do you want to restore to God that hardened heart like that of the pharaoh? Then you must go into the slums and bring them back to God, so that He can greatly reward you. Do you want to save sinners who are broken down under their sins? You also must be broken down. At least you must get near to them in their brokenness of heart and be able to sympathize with them. I believe that no man will command power over a person whom he does not understand either or know him. If you have never been to a certain place, you cannot know the road, but if you have been there yourself and you come upon a person who has lost his way, you are the man to direct him. When you have been through the same situation or circumstances that trouble others, you can say to them, "I have been there myself and I know all about it and the way to move forward from it." And you will tell them that by God's blessing, you will be able to conduct them out of the maze that they have found themselves in. You cannot pluck the brand out of the burning if you are afraid of being singed. You must be able and willing to dirty your fingers on the bars of the grate if you would do it. If there is a diamond dropped into a ditch, you must thrust your arm up to your elbow in the mud, or else you will not be able to pick the jewel out of the mire. The Holy Spirit, when He blesses a man, sets him down in the midst of the valley full of bones and causes him to pass by them and around them until he fully comprehends the greatness and the difficulty of the work to be accomplished.

Secondly, you must speak in the power of faith. Assuming Ezekiel had not had faith, he certainly would not have been able to preach to those dry bones—they made a wretched congregation. And he certainly would not have preached to the wind, for it must have been but a fickle listener. Who but a fool would behave in this manner unless religion entered into action? If preaching isn't a supernatural exercise, it's a useless procedure. God the Holy Spirit must be with you, or else you might as well go and stand on the tops of the hills of Scotland and shout to the east wind. There is nothing in all our eloquence unless we believe in the Holy Spirit making use of the truth which we preach for the quickening of the souls of men. Our prophesying must be an act of faith. We must preach by faith, as much as Noah built the ark by faith and just as the walls of Jericho were brought down by faith, men's hearts are to be broken by faithful preaching, that is preaching full of faith.

Thirdly, you must prophesy according to God's command. By prophesying, I do not mean foretelling future events, but simply uttering the message which you have received from the Lord, proclaiming it aloud so that all may hear. You will notice how it is twice said, in almost the same words, "So I prophesied as He commanded me." God will bless the prophesying that He commands, and not any other. So we must keep clear of that which is contrary to His Word and speak the truth which He has given to us to declare. Like Jonah, the second time he was told to go back to Nineveh was by the Lord to "preach unto it the preaching that I bid you," something that we must do if we would like to have our word believed in. Our message is received when it is accomplished by the Word of God through us. When the Lord describes the blessing that comes upon the earth by the rain and snow from heaven, he says, "So shall my word be that goes forth out of my mouth." Let us see to it that before a word goes out of our mouth, we have received it from the mouth of God. Then we may hope and expect that the people will also receive it from us. The Spirit of God—that is the breath of God—goes with the Word of God and with that alone.

Fourthly, we must break out in the vehemence of desire. Ezekiel was to prophesy to the dry bones, but he does not begin in a formal manner by saying, "Only the winds coming back will bring breath to those slain persons." No, he breaks out with an interjection and with his whole soul and mind heaving with a groundswell of great desire, he cries, "Come from the four winds, O breath, and breathe upon this slain, that they may live." He has the people before him in his eye and in his heart and he appeals, with mighty desire, to the Spirit of God that He would come and make them live. Today in our service, you will generally find that the men who yearn over the souls of their fellow men are those whom the Spirit of God uses more and more. A man of no desire gets what he longs for and that is nothing at all.

We must see only the divine purpose, the divine power, and the divine working. God will have His Spirit go forth with those who see His hand. "When I have opened your graves, O My people, and brought you up out of your graves, and then I shall put My Spirit in you, and you shall live, and that I shall place you in your own land: then shall you recognize that I, the Lord, have spoken it, and performed it," says the Lord. It is not our plan that God is going to work out but His own. It is not our purpose that the Holy Spirit is going to carry out but it is the purpose of the eternal Jehovah. It is not our power or our experience or our mode of thought which will bring men from death to life but it is the Holy Spirit who will do it and He alone. We must comprehend this fact and get to work in this spirit, and then God the Holy Spirit will be with us.

The Second Wind: Process Involved to Avoid Sinning Against It

The second wind (the wind of the Holy Spirit) possesses us and releases upon us spiritual blessings that we will never be deprived of. It crowns us with steadfast love and mercy. This wind releases upon us greater grace; so, therefore, we must avoid sinning against this wind. The processes involved in avoiding sinning against this wind shall thus be examined below.

The principle of applied kindness

We should be kind toward one another, both to those with whom we have a good relationship with and those whom, in one way or another, have offended us. This kindness was illustrated by Jesus on the cross in His dealing with the repentant thief. Earlier that day, the repentant thief had joined the other thief in mocking Jesus as He suffered on the cross. Then when the thief repented, Jesus responded to him with kindness. He was kind to the thief in spite of the way He must have felt at the time, and in spite of the thief's previous comments.

The principle of actively searching for barriers

The second principle that will help us avoid sinning against the second wind (wind of the Holy Spirit) is to actively examine our lives for things that would destroy us. Sins against the Holy Spirit are rarely committed in isolation from other sins. Most often, Christians tend to grieve the Holy Spirit in their abusive treatment of other Christians. Therefore, Paul realizes that the first step in restoring the previous intimacy with the Holy Spirit is searching out sin in our lives and repenting especially of those sins that have, in one way or another, hindered our relationship with other Christians.

The principle of forgiveness

This principle will help us overcome the tendency to grieve the Holy Spirit. We have to be compelled to forgive others "just as God in

Christ conjointly forgave you." Only as we come to understand just how offensive sin is to God can we begin to understand the immensity of His love in forgiving us. God demonstrates His own love toward us in how, while we were still sinners, Christ died for us; likewise, we also ought to express that love by forgiving others who have wronged us.

The principle of tenderheartedness

This principle implies that we should let our ways toward each other be characterized by tenderheartedness. The word "tenderhearted" suggests the idea of a heart full of compassion for others. Compassion for others was a motivating factor in the life of Jesus, and it should also motivate His followers in their dealings with others. When we begin to recognize hurting people and help them, it will change our attitude toward those who offend us and help us avoid sinning against the Holy Spirit.

The principle of deliberate steps

The principles of deliberate steps imply that we should walk with God in that which we do and desire to be like Him in our daily doing. Young children often desire to be like their parents or some other important persons in their lives. They will deliberately imitate the unique nature of their hero or role model. As Christians in the family of God, we, too, ought to desire to be like our Father in heaven and seek to imitate Him. Only as we yield and allow Him to live through us can we overcome the old nature and apply these principles to avoid sinning against the Holy Spirit.

Faith in Your Righteousness

We are a unit, a converted child of the living God. It's time we begin believing in the new birth and what Jesus has provided for us. You will realize that the Father has invited you to come boldly (confidently, without fear) to the throne of grace with your needs and requests. A Spirit created all matter, His name is Almighty God and He is our Father! The righteousness of God is what it's all about.

Folks, it is time to believe the Word of God. Did you know that there is no longer a sin problem? Jesus has solved our problems. He stopped the law of sin and death at the cross and in His resurrection. When we receive the salvation of God, we are put into the right standing with God and recreated by the Spirit of God as if sin had never existed. The only problem we have is the sinner problem. It is man's choice. All we need to do is choose righteousness and walk away from the sin problem. It is time to move in line with this revelation. We were sinners but we have been forgiven and we are now His workmanship, created in Christ Jesus. Let us begin to stand and believe in this instead of our past life. Our past life died the death of the cross. The Holy Spirit is the life force of God, and He lives in the heart of a believer. The force of righteousness completely overcomes the power of sin and death like how a bonfire overcomes a drop of water. We have more power over our lives—as the righteousness of God in Jesus Christ— than Satan had over us while we were in sin. As a believer, we must learn to depend on His free gift of righteousness. We must learn to lean on it.

When we discover who we are in Jesus, our entire existence, our health, our financial life, our social life will take on a new meaning. The storms of life will be stopped as we exert pressure on them with the Word of God and the power of the Holy Spirit dwelling within us. God sees us this way. He expects us to take our rightful place and live this kind of life above the beggarly elements of the world. God does not put these storms and rough spots before us, but He takes us through them and delivers us from them. God has given us the power and strength of the Holy Spirit and Jesus Christ as our Lord to change nations and governments around the world. Satan throws these things at us to stop us from acting on the Word and exercising our righteousness in Jesus Christ. Satan knows that these are dangerous spiritual weapons in the hands of a believer, so he is constantly trying to stop their effectiveness. Jesus said that when the spirit of truth comes, He would reveal the things of God to us. God, through the Holy Spirit, began to reveal to us the deep truths of the new birth, of the righteousness of God in Jesus Christ. He revealed the power of the Holy Spirit as that of God's muscle, God's mind, God's everything, and He showed how this part of the godhead was living inside every born-again, Spirit-filled believer. Then these truths became deeply rooted in our spirit. The Spirit of God has been sent into an earthly ministry just as legal and real as Jesus's earthly ministry. Jesus came to provide the way for us, and the Holy Spirit has come to teach us the way. Jesus came to fulfill the Abrahamic covenant and the Holy Spirit has come to make sure that the Christian covenant is fulfilled. The Spirit of God did not take the place of Jesus, but instead, because He is God the Holy Spirit, He has come to fulfill His own ministry as God the Father directed Him. The Almighty God is our very own Father. We are bone of His bone, the spirit of His Spirit, a joint-heir with Jesus Christ, and we are living in the kingdom of God. As we realize these things in our life, we become God-minded inside. We no longer think of God as being a million miles away because He is residing inside of us. The morality of God in Son is the drive behind our religion, causing us to triumph in His name. We, as believers, have the righteousness. We are the crowning creation of God. As reborn men, we are the greatest creatures in the universe. Man, in his natural, sinful state, was headed straight into hell. By the laws, he deserved to be condemned forever, but God, in His infinite mercy, intervened and legally changed the laws. He beat Satan at his own game, and life became the ruler over death. Jesus became the Lord and the champion of our salvation. He became the bishop over our souls in the new birth. He gave us His righteousness, the ability to triumph in His name, and we have peace with God. He was without sin but was made to be the sin. He was made to be our sinfulness so that we could be made in His righteousness. We have been made to sit with Him in heavenly places, in Christ Jesus, and victorious in Him! This is a real victory. We don't just bow a subservient knee to God, we join our faith with His, giving Him the opportunity to do a miracle in our hearts and turn us into the righteousness of Almighty God.

Conclusion

In summary, the wind of the Holy Spirit still made available for us today. The wind keeps our lives from going to waste. It crowns us with steadfast love and mercy. It indicates to us the love and will of God for our lives by helping us make perfect choices in life in whatever we do. It testifies of the truth so that we can make the best decision in life and fulfill our destiny. It brings us lasting happiness and eternal life and the reality of countless other essential gospels of truth. The wind makes us produce spiritual fruit and gives us access to the things of God. The wind makes the spirit dwell in us and makes us live in unity and peace with all men.

Chapter 9

The Wind of Blessing Declaration

The wind of blessing declaration is a wind of divine favor which gives us the prosperity and success with God. It is a special kindness shown toward mankind by God even when we do not struggle or labor for it. *"A good man obtaineth favour of the Lord: but a man of wicked devices will he condemn" (Proverb 12:2 KJV).* It is a wind of divine protection. It keeps us from harms or from being lost. It makes us not be afraid and cast out every fear. *"The Lord shall preserve thee from all evil: he shall preserve thy soul" (Psalms 121:7 KJV).* The wind is also a wind of praises to God for helping us in taking away our burdens and reproaches. *"Yet you are enthroned as the Holy one; you are the one Israel praises" (Psalms 22:3 NIV).* It is the wind of the fountain of joy that makes us enjoy the full redemption of salvation. It takes away every sorrow and pain we are facing. In it, we are delighted. *"Therefore with joy shall ye draw water out of the wells of salvation" (Isaiah 12:3 KJV).* The wind of blessing declaration bestows upon us the divine riches of God's kingdom. True riches are only committed to those whom God can trust. When you understand your covenant relationship with God, no economic circumstances can make you poor: *"Praise ye the Lord. Blessed is the man that feareth the Lord, that delighteth greatly in his commandments. His seed shall be mighty upon earth: the generation of the upright shall be blessed. Wealth and riches shall be in his house: and his righteousness endureth for ever" (Psalm 112:1–3 KJV).* It is a wind that makes us enjoy the divine health of God. Divine health is God's wish for us. The wind brings us out of every stronghold of sickness and diseases. It exempts us away from satanic assaults. It gives unto us the spiritual blood transfusion of the Holy Spirit: *"And when he was come into the house, the blind men came to him and Jesus saith unto them, Believe ye that I am able to do this? They said unto him, Yea, Lord. Then touched he their eyes, saying, According to your faith be it unto you. And their eyes were opened; and Jesus straitly charged them, saying, See that no man know it" (Matthew 9:28–30 KJV).*

It is also a wind of good fortune in each of your days doing every one of your endeavors in life and ministry: *"And the Lord shall make thee plenteous in goods, in the fruits of thy body, and in the fruit of the cattle, and in the fruit of thy ground, in the land which the Lord sware unto thy fathers to give thee. The Lord shall open unto thee his good treasure, the heaven to give the rain unto thy land in his season, and to bless all the work of thine hand: and thou shalt lend unto many nations, and thou shalt not borrow" (Deuteronomy 28:11–12 KJV).* The wind of blessing declaration is also a wind that God uses to keep us safe from every danger of life we are facing. Daniel in the lion's den was kept safe from the lion devouring him. The three Hebrew children were also kept safe in the furnace of fire from burning to death: "Then the king commanded, and they brought Daniel, and cast him into the dens of lions. Now the king spake and said unto Daniel, Thy God whom thou servest continually, he will deliver thee. And a stone was brought, and laid upon the mouth of the den; and the king sealed it with his own signet, and with the signet of his lords; that the purpose might not be changed concerning Daniel. Then the king went to his palace, and passed the night fasting: neither were instruments of musick brought before him: and his sleep went from him. Then the king arose very early in the morning, and went in haste unto the dens of lions. And once he came to the den, he cried with a lamentable voice unto Daniel: and the king spake and said to Daniel, O Daniel, servant of the living God, is thy God, whom thou servest continually, able to deliver thee from the lions? Then said Daniel unto the king, O king live forever, My God hath sent his angel and hath shut the lion's mouths, that they have not hurt me: forasmuch as before him innocency was found in me; and also before thee, O king, have I done no hurt" (Daniel 6:16–22 KJV).

Benefits of the Wind of Blessing Declaration

The wind of blessing declaration makes available to us the following:

1. Gives unto us the divine prosperity and provision from God— *"And my God shall supply every need of yours according to his riches in glory in Christ Jesus" (Job 22:21 ASV).*
2. Bestow on us the riches and wealth of the kingdom—*"I will give you the treasures of darkness And the hidden riches of secrets places, that you may know that I, the Lord Who call you by your name, Am the God of Israel." (Isaiah 45:3 NKJV)*
3. Makes us sing a new song.

The Blessings of God Working Wonders in Us

The blessing of God is upon humanity for this is a time of Revelation. This is the time when humanity is given an excellent gift, a great gift to give it purpose and direction facing the difficult and uncertain times ahead. This is the time through when humanity receives a broader understanding of his spirituality, a call for its unity and cooperation and its destiny both within this world and the world beyond within a greater community of intelligent life in the universe. God has placed at intervals in everyone the seed of data in order that this career could also be seen. This knowledge could be a larger intelligence at intervals in everyone and waiting to be discovered, but its whole existence is in relationship with the Creator of all life.

We may pray to God for many things. We may ask to be preserved. We may pray for opportunity and advantage. We may pray for the well-being of our family members and loved ones. But there is no greater responsibility that you could give and there is no greater gift that could be given than the blessing. For the blessing responds to a far greater question that comes from within you, from the need of your soul. It is a communication way on the far side, out of the reach of the intellect or the requirements of the instant. It is a way. It is a path. It is awareness. It is a journey. It is a mountain to climb. That is the blessing. It is the blessing of God that rearranges our life and gives it meaning. It is what will organize our thinking and give us an escape from ambivalence and chaos. This, regardless of our situations, will bring the blessing into our life, so that others can see it and feel it and respond to it. It is intangible. It is ineffable. Yet it has the power to bring all the greater rewards into our life. It is only the blessing that prepares and protects us. It is only the blessing that gives us the pathway through the uncertain and difficult times ahead. And it is only the blessing that prepares us for the Greater Darkness that is in the world the Greater Darkness that has the power to determine the future of every person and each future person in this world.

Our decisions and actions must follow the blessing and not precede it. We must allow ourselves to receive the gift of the blessing and then, step by step, we will know what to do what series of actions we must undertake, the thresholds that we must pass through, and the change that we must bring about in our own thinking and our own situation. Action and understanding follow the blessing. To give, we must first receive. To know, our eyes must first be open. To have the power and the courage to respond, we must see the need and feel the greatness of the times in which we live. We must prepare our mind and our emotions. We must prepare ourselves to receive the blessing and to experience the greater response within us, the great calling to the knowledge within us. We must allow this knowledge to emerge slowly, without trying to control it or dominate it or manipulate it in any way. God's blessing is the sole blessing that counts each for time and eternity. If you gain and die with the world's blessings, but lack God's blessing, woe to you! You are poor indeed! If we live and die with God's blessings, even though we lack what the world calls "blessing," we are truly blessed!

God's hand of blessing was upon Ezra and through God's hand of blessing upon him, the pagan king granted him all he requested. The king's grant is expressed within the letter that he gave to Ezra. The king granted him five things: (1) he authorized Ezra to go to Jerusalem and ensure that God's law was both taught and observed; (2) he provided a generous grant to buy supplies and temple vessels for the temple worship; (3) he commanded the treasurers in the provinces to supply anything that Ezra needed—up to 3¾ tons of silver, 600 bushels of wheat, 600 gallons of wine, 600 gallons of olive oil, and salt without limit; (4) he exempted all temple officials and workers from taxation; and (5) he authorized Ezra to set up a judicial system to see that all these laws were obeyed and that those who violate the laws were properly punished. Sometimes we miss the blessings of God because we fail to put God's purpose, priorities, and plans. Blessings are also missed because people fail to remember God's will, words, and ways. God has the ability to withhold His blessings to the disobedient.

Ways of Missing God's Blessing

Discouragement: God's blessings are often missed when people wallow in their discouragements. Haggai helped the people overcome their inertia with a strong authoritative word from the Lord. It often takes listening to a person of God who inspires us to act and break out of our ruts. Haggai was a task-oriented leader, but God used him in a complementary fashion with Zerubbabel, a religious priestly authority. Haggai's major influence came not through a political position but through God's giftedness. He overcame excuses that were given about building the temple as there had been a delay for sixteen years.

Excuses: God's blessings are usually incomprehensible unless folks gain supernatural perspective. Haggai gave the people divine perspective on what was happening to them in terms of their economy, politics, and agriculture. When people are able to see their circumstances from the eyes of God, they are apt to reverse their course. Learn to use God's Word to head off excuses, discouragements, and detours that people may throw in your face.

Thinking less: God's blessings are missed when people think that the size of their work is too great. Haggai fired up the people to not wax and wane in their enthusiasm. He strongly promised God's strength, provision, and enablement as they trusted and obeyed His will. Haggai did not give complicated answers but simple solutions from above. Oftentimes, it is much better to just give God's wisdom than intellectually complicated answers to people's problems. This will often come from our own communion with God's Spirit. Just begin where you can and gradually, the provisions, guidance, and resources will be heaped upon you. As your days, your strength will be measured.

Lack of patience: God's blessings are often missed when people lack patience. We have to be patient so that after we all have done the will of God, we might receive the promise. Haggai taught the people that, in order to see the full blessings of God, they needed to not immediately look for blessings, but wait upon the Lord and He would eventually come through. Keep on asking, seeking, and knocking and the doors will be opened to you. Persistence, importunity, faithfulness in prayer, devotion, and obedience always yield God's great blessings.

Wrong thinking: People miss out on God's blessings when they think that some work is too small. No work of God is too small when it is done with His timing, His teaching, and His treasures. Let us rely on the Lord's power, people, and priorities as evidence that we are walking in the presence of God. May the mind of Christ our Savior live in us. His love and power controlling all that we do and say. And may His promise be sufficient for everything pertaining to life and godliness, so that we do not start to rely on our own insights. It is enough to know, do, and believe the will of God as we live and move and have our greatest blessings in allowing the life of Christ to flow through His people like some sort of a watercourse of living water. From the fullness of God's grace we have received one blessing after another. We have received the blessing of the Father, the blessing of the Son, and the blessing of the Holy Spirit.

Engaging God: The God of Grace

It is the grace of God that makes us great. We cannot go far in life without the grace of God. Our parents are only vehicles that God use to bring us into this world, so it does not matter if you have parents right now or you are an illegitimate child, humanly speaking. You cannot be limited or disadvantaged when you operate under the grace of God.

Mysteries are kingdom secrets revealed to us for personal exploits. We cannot go beyond what is revealed to us. It is what is revealed to us that reveals us to our world. That is why you must passionately pursue God to reveal to us what will enthrone us. It is what is revealed to us that makes us different from others. It is what is revealed to us that distinguishes us. There is a secret that God will reveal to us that will give us a place in destiny. Grace is a mystery; it is God's free gift; we can never merit it. Whatever looks like shame or reproach in your life, grace will turn it around. *"As it is written, Jacob have I loved, but Esau have I hated" (Romans 9:13 KJV).* What did each of them do in the womb?

What Then Is the Grace of God?

Grace is the love and mercy given by God. We were created by grace, chosen right from the point of our conception by grace, and you can only survive here on earth by grace. When you recognize the grace upon your life, you will never go through disgrace.

Divine assistance given to man for regeneration

The grace of God is released for a purpose—our salvation and sanctification. Grace turns your life around. *"But by the grace of God I'm what I am: and his grace that was presented upon me was not in vain; but I laboured more abundantly than they all: yet not I, but the grace of God which was with me" (1 Corinthians 15:10 KJV).* When people look at you, you do not look like it, but its grace that qualifies you. Grace brought you thus far; grace shall keep you in Jesus Name. *"So then it is not of him that willeth, nor of him that runneth, but of God that sheweth mercy" (Romans 9:16 KJV).*

How to Grow in God's Grace

By living a life that pleases God: "What shall we say then? Shall we continue in sin, that grace may abound...God forbid" (Romans 6:1 KJV). God would never ask you to do what He has not "engraced" you to do. You are like your Father, and so, He desires for you to walk up to His expectations. When the grace of God takes over your life, struggles end.

By increasing in knowledge: It is important to understand that we have to increase in knowledge. The more of God you know, the more you grow in grace. *"Grace and peace be multiplied unto you through the knowledge of God, and of Jesus our Lord..." (2 Peter 1:2 KJV).* The more we grow in knowledge, the more grace is available to us and the more God enthrones us.

By prayer: "Let us, therefore, come boldly unto the throne of his grace, that we may obtain mercy and find grace to help in time of need." (Hebrews 4:16 JUB). We generate grace in the place of prayer. You must remain in His presence in order to keep generating grace. It is only in the place of prayer that we can tap into what God has released for us for each day.

God Rewards Good Stewardship

God is a good rewarder of those who diligently served Him. This is a truth about God of which many Christians don't seem to be aware. He loves to reward us when we diligently seek His presence, His will, and His ways. He rewards good work, and He rewards good stewardship. God rewards us when we pray or fast or give to the poor. *"Now he who plants and he who waters are one, and each one will receive his own reward according to his own labor" (1 Corinthians 3:8 NKJV).* God is going to reward us one day for our behavior or our good works. But it is also true that God rewards us while we're still here on earth.

"So Jesus answered and said, 'Assuredly, I say to you, there is no one who has left house or brothers or sisters or father or mother or wife or children or lands, for My sake and therefore the gospel's, who shall not receive a hundredfold now in this time—houses and brothers and sisters and mothers and children and lands, with persecutions—and in the age to come, eternal life" (Mark 10:29–30 NKJV).

God expects us to be good stewards of His people whom He puts in our path. And as we've seen, He is a rewarder of good stewards. God is always mindful of our material needs. He wants us to take some of the seeds He's given us and eat it, but the rest He wants us to sow. He even adds a promise about that seed. God has all the resources of the universe at His disposal. At the same time, He sees poor people who need to be fed, willing missionaries who need to be equipped and sent, and churches that need to be built. That's why His eyes are roaming the earth, looking for faithful-hearted stewards through whom He can channel millions of dollars into His kingdom. God is after our hearts, and the evidence that He has our hearts is that we give rather than giving to receive; and we give because we want to bless people, help people, and enlarge the kingdom of God. This, rather than reward, is our primary motive. Nevertheless, when we give with pure motives and hearts for God, He will immediately reward us and increase us so that we can give even more. God's arrangement for us is quite simply to convey us our living. God desires that we have an abundant and full life. In other words, God wants to bless us. God receives the glory after we direct ours because of Him, because the One who likes to be tested during this realm.

The Seasons of Our Lives

The Lord is bringing us into a new season, a season of blessings, breakthrough, favor, and prosperity. God is ushering into our lives a new blow of wind that will supernaturally and wonderfully turn our lives around for the good of the kingdom. A season of destiny fulfillment, destiny upliftment, and destiny enlargement. We are going to experience these various seasons in our lives.

Season of abundance: The Lord is bringing us into a new season of abundance. We may have experienced many difficulties or fearful and dangerous experiences in the wilderness to teach us obedience and faith. We may have gone through a season of lack and mere survival. We may have lived in the wilderness and experience having just enough and barely getting that which we desire or want. But the Lord brings us out of the wilderness into a season of abundance and overflow where we will have more than enough to meet our needs and have plenty leftover to share with others in need.

Season of joy: The Lord is bringing us into a new season of joy. We may have experience in one way or another a season of sorrow and pain in the past. But the Lord is bringing us out of the season of sorrow into a season of joy and happiness. He will turn our captivity and fill our mouths with laughter. He will turn our mourning into dancing. He will turn our sorrow into joy. He will grant our petitions and remove the sorrow from our hearts.

Season of peace: The Lord is bringing us into a new season of peace. In one way or another, we might have experienced one season of struggle or battles in the past. But the Lord is bringing us into a new season of peace and rest. He is changing the season of trials and tribulations and granting us a season of rest and relaxation. He will grant us victory in our battles and grant us rest from our wars.

Season of favor: The Lord is bringing us into our new season of favor. God is going to remove from us every season of closed doors and a hardened hearts that we might have encountered in one way or another. The Lord is changing that season and He is bringing us into a new season of favor with God and man. This is the year of the Lord's favor. This favor of the Lord will open doors of opportunities and favor and promotion for us. This favor will cause the doors which were closed to us to open and it will cause the hearts that were hardened against us to soften and become tender toward us. The Lord will lift us higher and increase our honor, and comfort us for all the pain and agony that we may have experienced in the past.

Season of harvest: A new season of harvest we are going to enjoy in Christ Jesus. We may have sown our seeds faithfully and are waiting patiently for the harvest. We may have become weary of well-doing as we have not yet received the harvest. The Lord is bringing us into a season of harvest for all the seeds we have sown. Our prayers and giving and witnessing are seeds which will bring us a great harvest or blessing in our lives. The Lord will pour out a blessing on us that we will not have room enough to receive it. The Lord will grant us a great harvest of souls for the seeds of the gospel that we have sown in the harvest of people. The Lord will also cause the evildoers and the wicked to reap the harvest for all their evil deeds. God cannot be mocked and the evil man will have to reap what he has sown.

Season of intimacy: The Lord is bringing us into a new season of intimacy with Him. We might have drifted away from the Lord and have become lukewarm in our relationship with the Lord. But the Lord is bringing us into a season of intimacy with Him. As we repent our sins and failures and backslidings and turn to the Lord, He will draw closer to us and write His law in our hearts and enable us to walk in His ways. The Lord draws close to those who are humble and contrite in the heart before Him. Pride will never let us get close to God. As we live close to God, we will experience greater blessings in our lives. When we seek Him with all our heart, He will reveal Himself to us. He will fulfill His purpose in our lives. He will guide us in the way that is best for us. He will answer our prayers. He will make our lives fruitful and make us a blessing to others. He will use us for His glory.

Made for Increase

God has made you with the power and potential for increase. At creation, God blessed all people with the ability for an increase: *God blessed them and said, "Be fruitful and increase in number and fill the water in the seas, and let the birds increase on the earth" (Genesis 1:22 NIV).*

You are blessed with the potential for increase. An increase, however, requires a change of heart for a change of actions and a change of life with results. God gives us a prophetic word that is not automatic, it is conditional. In His kingdom, there are spiritual actions on God's part and there are natural actions on our part to ensure the fulfillment of the prophecy. God is all powerful but our faith is the key to release His unlimited power in our lives.

God has given us a great privilege to represent Him as His sons and daughters on earth. He blessed Adam and Eve with an increase to establish the earth as it is in the kingdom of heaven. Adam and Eve were God's kingdom ambassadors on earth to rule in their Father's business on earth. God's will for His kingdom on earth would require blessed (anointed and appointed) sons and daughters with the ability to prosper in God's will for their lives and for His kingdom.

God's blessing in our lives includes the release of power for potential and ability to create our world in His world, and with authority to rule our world in this world. Our increase will be for our sake and for His kingdom's sake. Your purpose is wrapped up in God's purpose for us and for His kingdom. God's "covenant increase" in our life is powerful. God blessed Abram and Sarah with covenant increase. They made a few mistakes and made some choices that could have crippled their increase, but God intervened in their lives every time to watch over His purpose and promise of covenant increase. The enemy will challenge the Word of the Lord for our increase. He does this every time when there is a period of waiting for its manifestation. Eve doubted the Word of the Lord. Abraham had to be encouraged by God on more than one occasion to keep believing the Word of the Lord. Sarah laughed at the Word of the Lord. Hope is the mother of faith and faith is the key to receiving an increase. Without faith in God and in His Word, we cannot receive an increase. Joshua's heart had to be restored to believe again. Joshua's heart had to be restored for the courage he once had when only he and Caleb believed. Joshua's strength had to be restored as Moses's greatest leader and warrior. God sometimes have to do a work of restoration for an increase. Faith is the key to us receiving all miracles from God and, indeed, it is by our faith that we are restored even when we fail. When the anointing of the Holy Spirit comes upon us, it will empower us with a new level of power and authority once we believe, confess, and receive the anointing for the increase will manifest in a new level of God's obvious presence in our life.

There is a preparation of the heart for an increase for amazing things, for out of the heart comes all the issues of life. This process is called consecration. This process involved the preparation of our spirit and soul for an increase. Consecration is a process of purification. All we need is to go through a process of consecration for an increase. The increase means a new level of faith for a greater you and a greater reality of manifested glory in your life. Consecration will purify your heart, motives, and actions for increased favor with God and with His people. In this process of consecration, you have to forgive. You need to forgive God for not coming through as we believed in the past. Abraham was frustrated with God after twenty years of waiting for the promise of his own son with Sarah, and he vented his frustration before God. But Abram had to forgive God. *"And Abram said, 'You have given me no children; so a servant in my household will be my heir" (Genesis 15:3 NIV).*

Repent: We need to examine ourselves and see if there is anything in our heart and our life that is affecting our relationship with God. If it is hurt, unforgiveness, sin, anything that erodes faith in God and blocks your confidence in His Word, repentance will bring an instant release for your increase. If you confess your sins or mistakes, God is ready to forgive you and cleanse you. Repentance must be a lifestyle.

Believe again: Believe again, have faith again in the Lord your God. Choose to trust in God regardless of past circumstances. This is your season for an increase. Believe in God and believe in the Word of the Lord.

Confess your new season of increase: Begin to confess when you begin to prepare for your increase; it will add value to your faith. This is my season of increase.

Prepare for your increase: Be practical with your faith. Do something in preparation for your new expectations. God told the people to prepare for their increase, be joyful that your increase is coming and be expectant. Begin to work your faith with some practical actions such as: write a plan for your increase, identify and list your goals, pray and revisit past attempts or relationships. Do what you can do and God will do only what He can do.

Conclusion

In conclusion, the wind of blessing declaration ushers us into the realm of divine lifting in that which we do. It rescues us or removes from us every danger of life. It makes us cultivate the attitude of praises and thankfulness to God, and gives unto the satisfaction of God's kingdom. Start now and let praises become the focus of your life in Christ, count every one of His blessings and don't forget them. He (God) has provided wonderful benefits for us as His children, don't miss out on them.